CROSS
SEEKERS

FOLLOWOLOGY

Followology @ Collegiate Ministry: Following Jesus in the Real World

Allen Jackson

LifeWay Press
Nashville, TN

About Allen Jackson

Allen Jackson is assistant professor of Youth Ministry at New Orleans Baptist Theological Seminary. Basically, he has the task of bending the minds of those who will bend the minds of today's youth. Prior to teaching for 15 years, he served various churches as youth minister. Allen has written extensively for youth and collegiate resources. He is married and the father of two children.

Editor: Art Herron
Production Specialist: Leanne B. Adams
Graphic Designer: Bob Redden

Printed in the United States of America

ISBN 0-7673-9083-0

Dewey Decimal Classification: 248.834
Subject Heading: College Students—Religious Life

Scripture quotations are from the Holy Bible, *New International Version*, copyright © 1973, 1978, 1984 by International Bible Society. Used by permission.

TABLE OF CONTENTS

I N T R O D U C T I O N

INTRODUCTION

Before you get any further along, allow your imagination to be jump-started. Write out a description of a follower of Jesus—sort of a profile of a disciple. Try not to simply describe Peter or Andrew or Bartholomew. But if you are tempted to use a first-century description, be sure to update it. What would a follower of Jesus look like as a college student? Jot down some characteristics they would need.

1.   4.

2.   5.

3.

Give your definition of discipleship.
Discipleship is:

"Following Jesus" is one of the simplest definitions of discipleship. It seems fairly simple and concrete. Young adults think beyond the concrete (out of sight, out of mind) with a more mature, abstract thought process involving possibility thinking. Young adults are able to deal with metaphors and comparisons; they have learned that not everything is literal. They can imagine and project themselves into desired situations. They can lose the concrete component of discipleship as well. The result is that we might have a "church life" where we express belief in God and worship Him, singing praises as if we could reach out and touch Him. Then we return to our "rest of the week life" in the real world where it seems much more difficult to reach out and touch God while struggling with studies, customers, or relationships.

This book is an attempt to help college students picture what it is like to follow Jesus by returning to the concrete thinking of childhood. What is it like to follow someone physically? What would it be like to follow Jesus physically? The first disciples had to choose daily to "really, actually, personally, in the flesh" follow Jesus. Each chapter in this book includes the story of a biblical person faced with such a choice. A contemporary case study introduces every chapter as well.

Throughout this book, you will find boxes called "Chat Rooms." Please don't dismiss them as another fill-in-the-blank busywork kind of exercise. Consider it more of a journaling exercise. Journaling might include recording your insights about Bible verses, writing out some of your prayers, or keeping up with a prayer list to see how God is working. Let's try one.

▲Chat Room▲▲▲▲▲▲▲▲▲▲▲▲▲▲

Describe the last time you followed anybody anywhere. It could have been as part of a caravan to a ball game, concert, or conference. It might even have been to follow your parents to college as they helped transport your life to campus. Write the story as a journal entry. Include as much detail as possible—the route taken, things packed, who traveled with you, who was in the vehicle you followed, stops taken, food eaten, and so forth.

What precautions were taken to make sure you didn't get separated from the person you were following?

▲▲▲▲▲▲▲▲▲▲▲▲▲▲▲▲▲▲▲▲

Chat Room Goes Global

Perhaps you will discuss the Chat Room questions with a group at your church or campus ministry. If you lead college students, be aware that the Chat Room questions do not necessarily have answers. Your input is valuable while guiding students to learn by thinking through

▶ ▶

INTRODUCTION

these issues. Maybe as a group, a particular issue or question raises discussion that requires further input. If you have Internet access, go to the CrossSeekers home page at: www.crossseekers.com.

Maybe you have a story that would be helpful to those of us trying to follow Jesus. The story, experiences, answered prayers, and even things that you have learned can be posted. Sharing God's moving in the lives of fellow followers strengthens the body of Christ. Allow interaction with the principles and obstacles of followology to "go global" through the web page. Imagine a group studying followology in Florida. They are discussing a particular issue and decide to post a story or a question. An individual in Vancouver is the only college student in her church. Suddenly, she has a group to bounce her stories off of—only they happen to live on the other side of the continent! Allow time with followology and the web to be a chance to meet and encourage—even pray online with—other followers throughout the world.

Followology 101

In his book, *Getting Ahead by Staying Behind*, John Kramp invented the concept of *followology* which he defines as "the study of following and what that experience can teach Christians about discipleship." This book is a companion piece, designed to accompany Kramp's book. Some paragraphs in this book are lifted directly from *Getting Ahead by Staying Behind*. (John said it was okay for me to do this, but you really shouldn't try it on a research paper!) He suggested some *principles for* and *barriers to* followology which will prove helpful to college students. I am indebted to John Kramp for suggesting the discipline of followology and for identifying the principles and obstacles. I highly recommend his book, especially if you are leading a group of students through *Followology @ Collegiate Ministry*. Individuals working through this book will be helped by John's descriptions of followology through his unique storytelling style.

Welcome Fellow Followologist

Let me welcome you as a fellow followologist. I have been interested in discipleship for as long as I have known Jesus. I wanted to know what I was supposed to do as a new Christian. I was given a Bible and told to read it. The stories of the people who wanted to know God fascinated me: Moses, Abraham, Daniel, John the Baptist, Timothy. Then I heard about modern day followers like

- Jim Elliot, who lost his life witnessing to a primitive tribe;
- Watchman Nee, the imprisoned but passionate Chinese Christian writer;
- Lottie Moon, the diminutive missionary to China;
- Oswald Chambers, whose sermons were transcribed by his wife into the devotional classic, *My Utmost for His Highest*.

Their stories were great, but how could I be a disciple, too? How did I sign up without Jesus pointing at me and telling me that He would make me catch people? It seemed so distant, but I wanted to be a disciple. At first, I was interested because it sounded like a club or fraternity where I could belong. "I am a disciple"—it had a nice ring to it. Then I became involved in the youth group at the Pine Lake Baptist Church, where I observed that adults in the church acted like Jesus would probably act if He were teaching junior high Sunday School, singing in the choir, playing the organ or taking up the offering. I *saw* discipleship. I saw people in my life acting out their lives as followers of Jesus.

When I went to college, I found that I could be a member of a number of groups that advertised a discipleship program. Eventually, I "discipled" people, and I was "discipled" by other people. Those were significant times. Even then, I occasionally wondered: Am I really a disciple of Jesus, or am I just following the Christian crowd? Is discipleship a series of activities, or is it a relationship? If it is a relationship of following, is it a relationship following a significant leader during the college years, or is it following Jesus Himself?

I have found that the initial questions have to be addressed, or the discussion will produce "Sunday School answers." I see discipleship as a journey. College students are at a point where they are finally holding the reins, making decisions that determine the ultimate destination of their discipleship journey. My prayer is that this book will help you as you travel.

If you are studying this book alone, please take advantage of the web page to trade insights with other college students. If you are working your way through this book with a small group of other students, take your time. The number of chapters is designed to fit comfortably within a quarter, a semester, or a summer break. You may spend two weeks on a chapter, or you may take an extra week or two to gather feedback via the web page. If you are reading this workbook with a mentor, understand that this resource is not designed to teach to another. It is optimized as a group effort. *Please* don't be afraid to ask questions or to test out new ideas. We serve a big God who has patiently allowed questions for many millennia.

And Special Thanks to a Few

In addition to my gratitude to John Kramp for the whole idea behind followology, I appreciate the vision of Art Herron and the folks at National Student Ministry of the Baptist Sunday School Board. They gave me the opportunity (though not enough time) to tackle this project, then they edited the mess that I submitted. Thanks also to the campus ministers who met on the campus of the New Orleans Baptist Theological Seminary and conceptually shaped this book, even giving it the title! Stephanie Wright, my secretary at NOBTS assisted with the research, and the college group at First Baptist Church of Picayune, Mississippi, assisted with my perspective. My own children Aaron and Sarah constantly remind me that I am followed as a follower—and it startles me

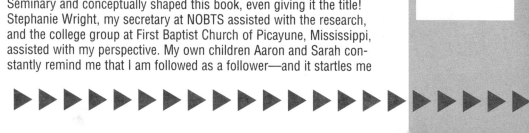

to think about the implications of the example that I provide.

I cannot write anything without the love and support of Judi, my bride and fellow follower.

Allen Jackson

Principles of Followology

In *Getting Ahead by Staying Behind,* John Kramp identified several components of the discipline of followology. He called these *followisms,* and he identified 24 followisms. They are listed, but you will not necessarily touch on them all in this workbook. If you see the term *followism,* you will know what I am talking about. The first chapter following this introduction is a section of Kramp's book.

The Twenty-Four Followisms

1. You can learn a lot by following.
2. Anyone can follow.
3. Following is a simple process.
4. Following is important.
5. If you don't know the way, you should follow the leader.
6. Following begins with an initial choice.
7. Following requires focus.
8. Following requires continual adjustment to the leader.
9. Following builds relationships.
10. Following changes followers.
11. Followers go where their leaders are going.
12. If you're the follower, you're not the leader.
13. Followers always need their leaders.
14. People follow in different ways.
15. Sometimes it's hard to follow.
16. Testing while following enhances learning.
17. Those who fail can follow again.
18. You can follow the leader without seeing the leader.
19. You can follow the leader by following the leader's written directions.
20. You can follow the leader by listening to the leader's voice.
21. The better you know the leader, the easier it is to trust the leader.
22. When it's dark, stand still and trust the leader.
23. You can help others follow as you follow the leader.
24. Following Jesus makes life meaningful.

CrossSeekers icons appear throughout this book. Each icon represents one of six principles for covenantal living based on the CrossSeekers Covenant. As you work through this book, if you are interested in learning more about CrossSeekers and how they are becoming followologists, contact us at our website: www.crossseekers.org.

C H A P T E R   O N E

FOLLOWING A LEADER YOU CANNOT SEE

Jamie was a senior in high school. Up to this point, the entire senior year had been a blast. Sure, classes were tough, but with the end in sight, he could do anything. What a fall season! Football games, marching band, fall carnival, the state fair, homecoming—as a senior, Jamie was on top of the world.

No major event caused the change. It was just that during Christmas holidays, the calendar turned over another year. Now the year matched the one on his class ring, and the finality of the end of high school became very real.

Now he realized that each activity was the last he would do with his high school friends. The last Valentine's Day dance, the last spring break, the last season he would put on his high school baseball uniform. The cockiness that comes with being a senior was being replaced with an uncertainty about the future. In high school, life was so scripted. You simply did what last year's senior class did at this time of year and that was that—like a game of follow the leader, even though the leaders were

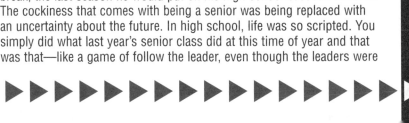

in college now. It had not occurred to Jamie until now that he *was* one of the leaders. But who would he follow?

Jamie had become a Christian in ninth grade. A lot of kids in the youth group had become Christians when they were six or seven years old. Sometimes he felt like he was behind on all the Bible stories and verses. Oddly enough, even those who had "walked the aisle" when they were much younger were rediscovering their faith. New questions popped up in Bible study. Hard questions—questions children would not ask. Questions like:

- Is the truth always the truth?
- What exactly does it mean that the Bible is inspired by God?
- How do I know that prayer really works?
- Are all religions alike?
- Can I make God mad? What happens if I do?

Those public questions made Jamie ask himself other questions when no one else was around:

- Does God really care where I go to college?
- If I occasionally doubt God's existence, does that mean I am not a Christian?
- Does God understand my desire for physical intimacy?
- Is there only one right girl for me to eventually marry?
- What does it mean to be called to ministry?

SPIRITUAL
GROWTH

In his "getting-ready-to-go-to-college world," it seemed to Jamie as if the whole church thing was separate from the rest of life. Jamie was relatively successful in his studies, his jobs, and his relationships. Sometimes he wondered if it was because he tried to follow Jesus, or if it was because he was just a good guy who worked hard.

Jamie was familiar with the stories of the early disciples. Jesus would tell them to do something or go somewhere, and they would. They didn't understand everything, but Jesus would explain it to them so they could understand. Following Jesus must have been easier when they could see Him physically. Jamie thought it was a lot harder today—to follow a leader who couldn't be seen.

▲Chat Room▲▲▲▲▲▲▲▲▲▲▲▲

Have you ever had thoughts like Jamie had about God?
❏ Yes   ❏ No   ❏ Never thought about it

Who is the "leader" you would go to in order to ask such questions?

If the answer is "Jesus," how do you know He hears you? List three ways.

1.

2.

3.

Think about what it takes to have your questions answered and get on with your discipleship journey. Pause for a moment! Think about it. If you feel comfortable sharing with someone else, please do.

▲▲▲▲▲▲▲▲▲▲▲▲▲▲▲▲▲▲▲

Following a Person

As you pondered the last question in the Chat Room, did you catch the word *journey?* Though you will continue to have questions about your walk with God (probably for the rest of your life!), there comes a time when you accept that there will be questions. Some of your questions will be answered in time, and some will have to wait until you can ask Jesus (in heaven).

Like Jamie in the case study, you may occasionally wish that you could follow Jesus physically—you know, hang around Him in person for a few days. The first disciples had that privilege, yet it blinded them to another kind of following. *The possibility of following Jesus some other way besides physically made their brains lock with confusion.* He told them flat out that they would have to learn to follow spiritually (like we have to) instead of physically (like they were used to). "But I tell you the truth: It is for your good that I am going away. Unless I go away, the Counselor will not come to you; but if I go, I will send him to you. When he comes, he will convict the world of guilt in regard to sin and righteousness and judgment; in regard to sin, because men do not believe in me; in regard to righteousness, because I am going to the Father, where you can see me no longer" (John 16:7-10).

> The possibility of following Jesus some other way besides physically made their brains lock with confusion.

Jesus made the future sound so simple. In essence, He described two types of following. In the first type of following, which we will call *Phase One,* the disciples had followed Jesus physically. In the second type *(Phase Two),* they would follow Him spiritually. In Phase One, they followed a leader they could see. In Phase Two, they would follow a leader they could not see. Thomas responded the same way that you and I probably would when Jesus announced that the paradigm was about to shift:

> "Do not let your hearts be troubled. Trust in God; trust also in me. In my Father's house are many rooms; if it were not so, I would have told you. I am going there to prepare a place for you. And if I go and prepare a place for you, I will come back and take you to be with me that you also may be where I am. You know the way to the place where I am going." Thomas said to him, "Lord, we don't know where you are going, so how can we know the way?" Jesus

answered, "I am the way and the truth and the life. No one comes to the Father except through me" (John 14:1-6).

▲Chat Room▲ ▲ ▲ ▲ ▲ ▲ ▲ ▲ ▲ ▲ ▲ ▲

If you were Thomas, what questions would you ask of Jesus as follow-up after He answered your first one? List two questions which come quickly to mind.
1.
2.

Think back to your high school graduation. As you said goodbye to some of your close friends, describe the feelings that accompanied the farewell. (A word will do.)

Did you think that you might never see some of the people again?
❑ Yes   ❑ No   ❑ Didn't think about it

Stretch here. Is it possible the disciples had an awful feeling in the back of their minds that they would never see Jesus again?

▲▲▲▲▲▲▲▲▲▲▲▲▲▲▲▲▲▲▲▲

See the Leader? I Can't Even Get Online!

How can we follow when we cannot see? Just as the disciples were blinded because they had not known anything except Phase One (physical) following, we might be blinded because we have never known anything but Phase Two (spiritual) following. Intellectually, we can affirm that it is possible to follow a leader we cannot see. In reality, we occasionally must admit that our relationship with Jesus takes a back seat to other factors in determining daily life choices. In the physical realm, the relatively primitive communication offered by walkie talkies or CB radios demonstrates this reality. The potential to communicate was there, but the transmissions were rarely without problems. An event that occurred more recently illustrates further.

In the late 1990s, the Internet became available to common people like you and me. Many colleges and universities began to provide an email address to any enrolled student. As a student minister, email was a fantastic way to keep up with my college group. However, when the initial wave of Internet popularity began to roll in, access was generally available through online services like America Online, Prodigy, and Compuserve. As a promotional gimmick, America Online offered unlimited Internet access for a fixed monthly fee. They were unprepared for the

tremendous response, and the business was more than they could handle. The result was that a whole bunch of people signed up for Internet access through AOL, but then they found they could not go online because of the telephone traffic volume. Their attempts to surf the net were beached by a busy signal. Consider some of the physical limitations that would-be Internet users faced:

• *Limited capacity to communicate*—they would sit and stare at the little hourglass only to be told they couldn't connect. They would feel powerless with the endless, "no carrier detected" messages.

• *Inability to overcome interference*—other callers got in ahead. There were just not enough telephone lines to handle everyone. The height of frustration came when they finally did connect, but forgot to disable call waiting. Just as they wanted to check email, they would get blown away by an incoming call.

• *Inability to receive transmissions*—someone would say, "Did you get my email?" and the response would be, "I haven't been able to get on AOL."

In our Phase Two following, we may feel similar spiritual limitations in our ability to communicate with God:

• *Limited capacity to communicate with Jesus.* We wonder if we can have a real relationship with Jesus if we can't see Him and cannot be with Him physically. At times, we question if we have the spiritual equipment required to connect us to Jesus.

• *Inability to overcome interference.* Can our feeble spiritual systems overcome the busy signals so we can communicate with God? Is it possible that He is busy with other callers and that He will take our call in the order in which it was received? Does it sometimes seem as if Christians we deem more spiritual can get through, while we cannot?

• *Limited capacity to receive transmissions.* Even with our modems on and set to receive, we still wonder if God's transmission can reach us. Does He actually speak to us? If so, how can we get to the mail He has left in our box?

The Decision Is to Decide

We began this chapter acknowledging that hard questions may arise in the minds of young adults (and older ones, too!) concerning God's nature and activity. Study the lives of biblical persons like Abraham, Jacob, Job, and Jeremiah, and you will see that God is okay with the questions. In the New Testament, all of the disciples struggled at times with believing that Jesus would answer all their questions. Each of the persons in the biblical record made a critical decision, however. *They made a conscious decision to follow God.* As an act of their will, based on a faith in an unseen God, they purposefully began the journey of discipleship. You cannot be a disciple unless you make such a decision. Stop reading now. Find a quiet place if you are not in one already. In the space below, write out a prayer telling God you have decided to be a disciple in spite of questions you may have.

Phase Two following involves a willingness to get on with the journey of discipleship as followologists—in spite of our doubts. And what a journey it is!

The Joy of the Journey

As a youth minister in a large city, I sensed the need to get our youth group out of the city for a spring retreat. For something different, the retreat (called "Truth Trek") was to be held along the Appalachian Trail in North Georgia. The unique aspect of this retreat was that the hike *was* the retreat. The value was in the journey, not in the destination. If we focus so much on having all of our doubts settled and all of our questions answered, we miss the molding and shaping God does with each of us along the way. *The process of discipleship is as important as the product, that is—disciples.*

> The *process of* discipleship is as important as the *product,* that is—disciples.

Eugene Peterson wrote one of my favorite books that touches on the idea of discipleship as a journey. In *A Long Obedience in the Same Direction*, Peterson examines Psalms 120—134, the 15 psalms labeled "Psalms of Ascent." So named because the destination city of Jerusalem is geographically elevated, the psalms were used as "road music" by the Jewish pilgrims who traveled to Jerusalem for the various festivals observed by the Israelites. The psalms were sung during the trip and represent many aspects of the faith journey: repentance, worship, security, joy, perseverance, humility, and obedience. The way we view ourselves as travelers on the journey significantly impacts the richness we find along the way. Peterson identifies two concepts used to describe people on the faith journey:

> In going against the stream of the world's ways there are two biblical designations for people of faith that are extremely useful: disciple *(mathetes)* says we are people who spend our lives apprenticed to our Master, Jesus Christ . . . . A disciple is a learner, but not in the academic setting of a schoolroom, rather at the work site of a craftsman.
>
> Pilgrim *(parepidemos)* tells us we are people who spend our lives going someplace, going to God, and whose path for getting there is the way, Jesus Christ . . . Jesus, answering Thomas's question, "Lord, we do not know where you are going; how can we know the way?" gives us directions: "I am the way, and the truth, and the life; no one comes to the Father, but by me" (John 14:5-6).[2]

If someone says, "Just follow me" (and you actually follow), it indicates that you are trusting someone else to lead you on a kind of journey. I live in a part of New Orleans where it is not a great idea to be lost. Sometimes when someone comes to visit, I meet them at the interstate and allow them to follow me to my house. Their responsibility for navigation ended when they got off the interstate. From that point on, they watch the taillights of my Honda and trust me to find my driveway. They may have questions about some of the things they see as they journey to my house, but they don't put on the brakes and refuse to follow because of those questions.

▲Chat Room▲▲▲▲▲▲▲▲▲▲▲▲▲▲

List a person you followed physically during the course of a semester. How did you follow them? Why did you follow them?

Person followed: _____

How followed: _____

Why followed: _____

List a person you followed spiritually during the course of a semester. How did you follow them? Why did you follow them?

Person followed: _____

How followed: _____

Why followed: _____

Different Types of Following

In the Bible, the word follow is used about a gazillion times. Often, it is used to describe the concept of following commandments or laws. Look up these verses. Identify what was to be followed. (See if you can describe it in one word.)

Psalm 119:33

Psalm 119:63

Psalm 119:106

Psalm 119:166

Jeremiah 13:10

Jeremiah 23:10-17

Ezekiel 20:13-21

▲▲▲▲▲▲▲▲▲▲▲▲▲▲▲▲▲▲▲▲

►►►►►►►►►►►►►►►►►►►►►

In the New Testament, the idea of following is almost always that of following a person. The idea behind followology is that of following a person. As disciples, we are following a person. And that person is Jesus.

Imagine this scene. You are a fisherman who makes a living from the sea. Each day, you fish. You understand nets and hooks and boats and bait. One day, early in the morning, a man who preaches comes up to you and tells you how to fish. You roll your eyes, give your fishing buddies the "who made this guy the fishing show host?" look and continue to listen to the preacher. You figure he knows about preaching, but you know fishing. Just to humor him (you have met him before and have seen him do some pretty special things), you follow his instructions, and the result is that you catch more fish than you have ever caught. Then he says that you will fish for people from now on, and that you are to follow him. For some reason, it makes perfect sense. So you follow.

The disciple in the paragraph is Peter. Each of the disciples was challenged to follow Jesus physically. They could see Him, they could touch Him, they could observe the miracles Jesus accomplished. Like Jamie in the story above, it seems like it would be easier if Jesus showed up in your dorm room and performed a miracle or two. (Jesus, how about starting with my GPA? Just kidding!) After you had been convinced He was different from all of the other "prophets" on campus, He would challenge you to leave school and follow Him. And then . . . well, maybe it wouldn't be that easy. Let's pause to think about it.

Following for Good

Unlike the experience of following people who pop into your room and say, "Come with me to Wal-Mart," or "Let's go grab a burger," when Jesus calls us to follow, we leave for good. With friends who drop in, we know we are coming back. The journey doesn't require much commitment. When I left home for college with all my earthly possessions in my car, I knew that I still had a place at my parents' home. As an adult, when I moved my family from one state to another, I had a feeling of commitment that came along with the knowledge that I wouldn't be coming back. Jesus called the disciples to leave and physically follow (Mark 1:14-20). They did not know how long the journey would be or where they would go.

We know Jesus has gone to be with God. Yet He has not left us alone on our journey. As God gave the Jewish pilgrims some Psalms to remind them of His presence, so He has left us the Bible, the Holy Spirit, and the promise that spiritual following is even better. In John's Gospel, the writer recorded the words Jesus told His disciples about us: "Then Jesus told him, 'Because you have seen me, you have believed; blessed are those who have not seen and yet have believed'" (John 20:29).

To help us in our journey, He has left us written instructions (the Bible), the thrill of the promise that we will hear His voice, guidance when we get temporarily disconnected, and even the assurance that He will not leave us when we feel totally lost and unable to follow at all.

God's Onscreen Help

I remember the first word processing program for my computer. It came with two different manuals, each one over two inches thick. To navigate the program, I had to have the manual close at hand in case I wanted to learn a new feature or in case I locked up the program. Few computer programs come with a manual any more. All the help features as well as the tutorials are on screen, built into the program. My children have a computer program that allows them to "pick a friend" who will guide them through the program. They are shown the pictures of six children, each with their own voice. When my daughter chooses the "friend" that she will play with on the computer that day, the voice of the friend guides her through the various components of the program.

Isn't it amazing that the people who wrote the software could antici-pate problems we would have, questions that would arise, and even predict ways we would use the program? Even more amazing is the thought that thousands of years ago God could anticipate problems we would have, questions that would arise, and even predict ways we would go though life. *His help feature is called the Bible.*

> **His help feature is called the Bible.**

As Jesus prepared His disciples for Phase Two following, He stressed the importance of His "Word"—all that He said and taught. He expected the disciples to listen and to apply His teaching to their lives. Jesus wanted them to understand that when they did what He said, they were following Him. They were to listen to Jesus' spoken words and act on them. Fortunately, we were given those words in writ-ing.

Jesus knew that His words would be written down for us and for all future followers to read, study, and apply to their lives. Unlike any other collection of religious writings, the Old and New Testaments would become the perfect spiritual road map to help disciples navigate life.

▲Chat Room▲▲▲▲▲▲▲▲▲▲▲▲▲

Consider the following verses. Rewrite each one (use your own lan-guage—slang is okay) as a personal note to you from God. Follow with a journal entry containing your response to that Scripture. Allow it to apply specifically to your life as a college student or young adult.

All Scripture is God-breathed and is useful for teaching, rebuking, correcting and training in righteousness, so that the man of God may be thoroughly equipped for every good work (2 Tim. 3:16-17).

►►►►►►►►►►►►►►►►►►►►

My Interpretation:

▲▲▲▲▲▲▲▲▲▲▲▲▲▲▲▲▲▲▲▲▲▲▲▲

> I imagine that a Phase One follower would be stunned to hear that in 2000 years, Jesus' words would be so widely available... They would probably say, "Wow, Dude!"

I imagine that a Phase One follower would be stunned to hear that in 2,000 years, Jesus' words would be so widely available that in some parts of the world people would have five or six copies. On top of that, there would be songs written and recorded to help magnify Jesus' words. Posters, bumper stickers, computer reminders, FAX documents—Jesus' words would be found everywhere. *They would probably say, "Wow, Dude!"*

[Wonder: How you would say this in Greek text?]

Even with all the tools to help us—in spite of all of the communication technology, including Christian publishing—there is a crisis today in biblical literacy. One of the commandments for van travel with youth groups is that every single van in the caravan has a written set of directions and a road map in it. Even if they plan to stay together, one or more vans always gets separated. The written instructions give the wayward van a chance to get back in the pack and reach the final destination.

Many Christians have gotten a bit separated from the pack and have lost their spiritual maps (or do not know how to read them). Sadly, inside and outside the church, people are uninformed, confused, or both, about the words in the Bible. Not only do the finer points of theology puzzle them, but the central truths of the Christian faith jumble in their minds.

For the entire history of the Bible, God has used the Holy Spirit to help people understand what God wanted us to know. The Holy Spirit inspired the original writers. The Holy Spirit inspired those who decided which books to include and which books to leave out. The Holy Spirit has protected the authenticity of each translation through the centuries. And Jesus promised that the Holy Spirit would help us use the Bible to stay on course. The Holy Spirit *does not* download a giant biblical file into our heads and, poof! we are better followers. It is our responsibility to read and understand the Bible. If we want to deepen our walk with Christ, we should follow these essential steps:

• *Know the story.*—Beginning with the story of Jesus as recorded in the Gospels, we need to know the basics of the Bible. Perhaps as a study for a small group in your college ministry, you would take on a series of the great stories in the Bible that reveal God's hand in history. For example, in successive weeks, your group might study:

CHAPTER ONE

- the creation
- the human fall
- the introduction of sin into the world
- the exodus
- the burning bush
- Joseph and his brothers
- David and Goliath
- Elijah and the prophets of Baal
  and that is just the Old Testament!

• ***Understand the Story.***—It is important that we move beyond basic facts and strive to understand what is said. Use this formula for understanding.

1. What are the actual words saying (define any that are unclear)?
2. What was the meaning for the original hearers or readers?
3. What is the meaning for me today?
4. What should change about my life as a result of understanding this passage?

• ***Interpret the Story.***—We do great harm when we pick individual verses out of context in order to build a system of thought for ourselves. In addition to consulting reputable commentaries and other reference materials, pastors, Bible teachers, and others can help us to correctly interpret the more difficult passages.

• ***Accept the Whole Story.***—Thomas Jefferson constructed his own Bible by cutting out sections he didn't understand or agree with. The total biblical message is our spiritual map. We must not set aside those passages which are difficult or which cause us to realize we cannot leave our lives the way they are and still be aligned with God's Word. John Stott said it this way:

> What is the major reason why evangelical Christians believe that the Bible is God's Word written, inspired by his Spirit and authoritative over their lives? . . . the overriding reason for accepting the divine inspiration and authority of Scripture is plain loyalty to Jesus. . . . Our understanding of everything is conditioned by what Jesus taught. And this everything means everything: It includes his teaching about the Bible. We have no liberty to exclude anything from Jesus' teaching and say "I believe what he taught about this but not what he taught about that."[3]

▲Chat Room▲▲▲▲▲▲▲▲▲▲▲▲▲▲

To whom do you answer (from an authority standpoint) and why? Jot it down.

With regard to written instructions, are you a. . . (check one)
- person who studies directions and carefully applies them?
    ❏ Yes   ❏ No
- person who scans the directions and does your best?

❑ Yes   ❑ No
- person who digs directions from the trash as trouble occurs?
❑ Yes   ❑ No
- person who is in serious trouble if there are no pictures?
❑ Yes   ❑ No

On a scale of 1-10, with 10 being the maximum, rate how much you believe the Bible is helpful in directing your daily life.

List three ways the Bible could be like a road map.
1.
2.
3.

▲▲▲▲▲▲▲▲▲▲▲▲▲▲▲▲▲▲▲▲▲

Students often ask how to know God's will. I respond sometimes with this formula (completely non-scientific and only my opinion): 98% of God's will is in the Bible. If it is not plainly stated in Scripture, another 1.5% of God's will can be discovered through common sense or wise counsel of Christian friends. If one still hasn't discovered God's will, then God will provide a divine revelation. Divine revelations are valid, but they must remain secondary to and be consistent with the biblical revelation.

A college student claimed God had told him he was to marry a certain girl. He expected that she (and her boyfriend at the time) should pay attention to what God had told him. The problem was, God had not yet informed the girl of the plan. God will not say anything today through any subjective means that contradicts what He has already said in the Bible. In the situation above, I reminded him that God made sure that both Mary and Joseph were instructed as to the events surrounding Jesus' birth. The Word is available to every follower as a map for discovering God's will.

Calling Technical Support

I ordered my wife a notebook computer through a magazine this year. It has all the new stuff on it (I am writing this on a 486 x 33 notebook computer about to celebrate its fourth birthday, which is like 120 in computer years). I will eventually make the jump from Windows 3.1 to Windows 95, or 97, or 00, or whatever version is the latest. As a matter of fact, the computer in my office at the seminary has the newer version. The trouble is, I don't know how to work it. I got really good at DOS in the early part of the '90s. I finally went to Windows because I had friends who would explain it to me. *Now I am supposed to try something else?* To try to understand this new world, and not wanting to bother my friends, I called technical support. I wanted to ask what I needed to do to upgrade my program.

> Now I am supposed to try something else?

I may be old-fashioned, but when I call a technical support line, I would like to talk to someone who has patience with me. I do not particularly like to be told that there is a 45 minute wait time to speak to a real person, but that I can receive the help I need by finding the web page or by having them FAX me a document. Worse yet, I am afraid of getting a real person on the line and having them understand that I have trouble with new programs.

This story was passed around via email. Whether it is true or not, I don't know, but sometimes I feel like the caller in the story:

Actual dialog of a former WordPerfect Customer Support employee:

"Ridge Hall computer assistant; may I help you?"

"Yes, well, I'm having trouble with WordPerfect."

"What sort of trouble?"

"Well, I was just typing along, and all of a sudden the words went away."

"Went away?"

"They disappeared."

"Hmm. So what does your screen look like now?"

"Nothing."

"Nothing?"

"It's blank; it won't accept anything when I type."

"Are you still in WordPerfect, or did you get out?"

"How do I tell?"

"Can you see the C:\prompt on the screen?"

"What's a sea-prompt?"

"Never mind. Can you move the cursor around on the screen?"

"There isn't any cursor: I told you, it won't accept anything I type."

"Does your monitor have a power indicator?"

"What's a monitor?"

"It's the thing with the screen on it that looks like a TV. Does it have a little light that tells you when it's on?"

"I don't know."

"Well, then look on the back of the monitor and find where the power cord goes into it. Can you see that?"

"Yes, I think so."

"Great! Follow the cord to the plug, and tell me if it's plugged into the wall."

"Yes, it is."

"When you were behind the monitor, did you notice that there were two cables plugged into the back of it, not just one?"

"No."

"Well, there are. I need you to look back there again and find the other cable."

"Okay, here it is."

▶ ▶ ▶ ▶ ▶ ▶ ▶ ▶ ▶ ▶ ▶ ▶ ▶ ▶ ▶ ▶ ▶ ▶ ▶ ▶

"Follow it for me, and tell me if it's plugged securely into the back of your computer."

"I can't reach."

"Uh-huh. Well, can you see if it is?"

"No."

"Even if you maybe put your knee on something and lean way over?"

"Oh, it's not because I don't have the right angle — it's because it's dark."

"Dark?"

"Yes—the office light is off, and the only light I have is coming in from the window."

"Well, turn on the office light, then."

"I can't."

"No? Why not?"

"Because there's a power outage."

"A power . . . A power outage? Aha! Okay, we've got it licked now. Do you still have the boxes and manuals and packing stuff your computer came in?"

"Well, yes, I keep them in the closet."

"Good! Go get them, and unplug your system and pack it up just like it was when you got it. Then take it back to the store you bought it from."

"Really? Is it that bad?"

"Yes, I'm afraid it is."

"Well, all right then, I suppose. What do I tell them?"

"Tell them you're too stupid to own a computer."

I Want a Real Person Who Has Patience with Me!

I confess. Sometimes, I need to hear the voice of someone who loves me and who knows that I am not perfect and that I struggle with understanding things written in the Bible. I also confess that in a complicated world filled with noise, it is hard to hear the voices that are on my side, looking out for my best interests. When we are trying to follow someone, it takes concentration. Have you ever noticed that when you are driving around looking for someone's house or apartment, armed only with an address, that you almost always turn the music down in your car? Why? Because you need to concentrate on trying to find the person. Once you get on the right street or figure out the address sequence, you turn the tunes back up.

▲Chat Room▲ ▲ ▲ ▲ ▲ ▲ ▲ ▲ ▲ ▲ ▲ ▲

List four "voices" that give you instruction during a normal week.

1.

2.

3.

4.

Is one voice more important than another voice? Why? Jot down a word to describe why one voice is more important than the other.

Think about what the following verse has to do with listening to the right voice. Share it with a friend, if possible.

Jeremiah 29:11: "'For I know the plans I have for you,' declares the LORD, 'plans to prosper you and not to harm you, plans to give you hope and a future.'"

▲▲▲▲▲▲▲▲▲▲▲▲▲▲▲▲▲▲▲

I Want to Listen to a Real Person!

Jesus used the analogy of the shepherd to illustrate that His followers would be able to recognize His voice the way sheep recognize the voice of their shepherd:

> "The man who enters by the gate is the shepherd of his sheep. The watchman opens the gate for him, and the sheep listen to his voice. He calls his own sheep by name and leads them out. When he has brought out all his own, he goes on ahead of them, and his sheep follow him because they know his voice. But they will never follow a stranger; in fact, they will run away from him because they do not recognize a stranger's voice" (John 10:2-5).

The disciples were being prepared for Phase Two following. As Phase One followers, they heard Jesus' voice and physically followed. He was teaching them to follow a voice that belonged to a leader they could not see.

Another illustration involves my son. Occasionally, I will go to my office (which is about a quarter of a mile from my house) and leave my son and daughter home by themselves. They think this is cool. We have a routine for me to check on them. I will call the house. They are instructed not to answer the phone until they hear on the answering machine who it is. When they recognize my voice, they pick up the phone. Otherwise, they let the caller leave a message.

How do you know God's voice when you cannot see Him? The Bible is full of instances where followers heard God's voice. Adam, Moses, Samuel—all had to discern that the voice they heard was that of the God who loved them. Consider that of a young Samuel:

> The LORD called Samuel a third time, and Samuel got up and went to Eli and said, "Here I am; you called me." Then Eli realized that the LORD was calling the boy. So Eli told Samuel, "Go and lie

▶▶▶▶▶▶▶▶▶▶▶▶▶▶▶▶▶▶▶▶

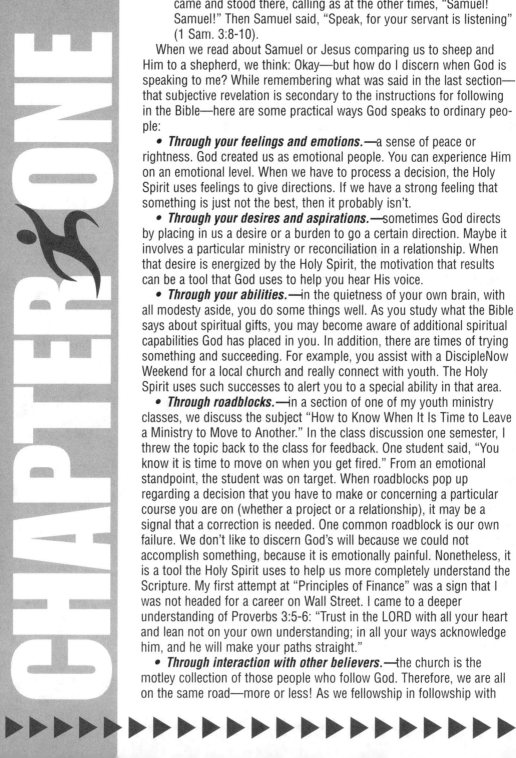

down, and if he calls you, say, 'Speak, LORD, for your servant is listening.'" So Samuel went and lay down in his place. The LORD came and stood there, calling as at the other times, "Samuel! Samuel!" Then Samuel said, "Speak, for your servant is listening" (1 Sam. 3:8-10).

When we read about Samuel or Jesus comparing us to sheep and Him to a shepherd, we think: Okay—but how do I discern when God is speaking to me? While remembering what was said in the last section— that subjective revelation is secondary to the instructions for following in the Bible—here are some practical ways God speaks to ordinary people:

• *Through your feelings and emotions.*—a sense of peace or rightness. God created us as emotional people. You can experience Him on an emotional level. When we have to process a decision, the Holy Spirit uses feelings to give directions. If we have a strong feeling that something is just not the best, then it probably isn't.

• *Through your desires and aspirations.*—sometimes God directs by placing in us a desire or a burden to go a certain direction. Maybe it involves a particular ministry or reconciliation in a relationship. When that desire is energized by the Holy Spirit, the motivation that results can be a tool that God uses to help you hear His voice.

• *Through your abilities.*—in the quietness of your own brain, with all modesty aside, you do some things well. As you study what the Bible says about spiritual gifts, you may become aware of additional spiritual capabilities God has placed in you. In addition, there are times of trying something and succeeding. For example, you assist with a DiscipleNow Weekend for a local church and really connect with youth. The Holy Spirit uses such successes to alert you to a special ability in that area.

• *Through roadblocks.*—in a section of one of my youth ministry classes, we discuss the subject "How to Know When It Is Time to Leave a Ministry to Move to Another." In the class discussion one semester, I threw the topic back to the class for feedback. One student said, "You know it is time to move on when you get fired." From an emotional standpoint, the student was on target. When roadblocks pop up regarding a decision that you have to make or concerning a particular course you are on (whether a project or a relationship), it may be a signal that a correction is needed. One common roadblock is our own failure. We don't like to discern God's will because we could not accomplish something, because it is emotionally painful. Nonetheless, it is a tool the Holy Spirit uses to help us more completely understand the Scripture. My first attempt at "Principles of Finance" was a sign that I was not headed for a career on Wall Street. I came to a deeper understanding of Proverbs 3:5-6: "Trust in the LORD with all your heart and lean not on your own understanding; in all your ways acknowledge him, and he will make your paths straight."

• *Through interaction with other believers.*—the church is the motley collection of those people who follow God. Therefore, we are all on the same road—more or less! As we fellowship in followship with other Christians, we can learn from them and join them to accomplish tasks we could not do alone. Often we hear God's voice through insights He gives to other believers. While we sometimes struggle to appreciate viewpoints of some other Christians, we still need to learn from them. I struggle at times with accepting the leadership of persons God has placed in authority over me, people like my boss, my pastor, and my accountability partner. Yet, if God in His wisdom placed them there, then His voice can be heard through their counsel.

What Would Jesus Do?

A popular bracelet being worn these days has the initials, *WWJD,* which stand for "What Would Jesus Do?" Based on the storyline in the book, *In His Steps* by Charles Sheldon, the phrase represents a commitment to evaluate every decision in light of what we think Jesus would decide if He were in the same situation. I would like to propose an amendment. What if we printed bracelets that had the initials *WDJD* which could stand for "What Did Jesus Do?"

As we follow a leader we cannot see, we are fortunate to be able to study what He did and said in the first century as recorded in the Bible. As Phase Two Followers, we can use our knowledge of Jesus' activities and priorities two thousand years ago to determine general principles that will help us follow Him now. Since Jesus is the same yesterday, today, and forever, we can anticipate that He will do today what He did then.

▲Chat Room▲▲▲▲▲▲▲▲▲▲▲▲▲▲▲

Discuss followism #21: The better you know the leader, the easier it is to follow. Before you talk about it as a group, perhaps individuals can search out some Scripture references that deal with knowing Jesus.

Here is an Old Testament verse to get you started: Psalm 46:10. According to this verse, what must we do to know God better? Find some examples of how Jesus did exactly that.

It's time to move on. I know all of your questions have not been answered. Nor will they be. You have, however, completed "Followology 101," which indicates you have decided to trust Jesus to help you better understand what it means to follow Him as you journey with Him. In the next chapter, you will look at a principle and a barrier involved with Following the One Who Knows the Way.

▲▲▲▲▲▲▲▲▲▲▲▲▲▲▲▲▲▲▲▲▲

CHAPTER ONE

Notes

1. Eugene Peterson, *A Long Obedience in the Same Direction* (Downers Grove, IL: InterVarsity Press, 1980), From the introduction.

2. Ibid., 13.

3. John R.W. Stott, *The Authority of the Bible* (Downers Grove, IL: InterVarsity Press, 1974), 7-8.

ARE YOU STILL FOLLOWING?

CHAPTER ONE

C H A P T E R   T W O

FOLLOWING THE ONE WHO KNOWS THE WAY

Followology Principle: The Need Principle determines our motivation for following.
Followology Barrier: Role Confusion (If you're the follower, you're not the leader.)

The big day had finally arrived. All the preliminaries were out of the way: SAT test, ACT test, blood test, shots. Marked "received" were the scholarship applications (with all those essays!), acceptance letters, and dormitory applications. Picking the college was easy compared to the

paperwork. It made Alexandra tired just to think about all the hoops she had jumped through just to make it this far. It was a lot of work, but everything had fallen into place. Even her roommate, Stephanie, was a perfect match. They were good friends, but not so close they couldn't have some space. The picture of the dorm room in the information brochure the university had sent helped them plan how to "make it their own place."

Now the departure checklist was complete. Matching bedspreads and curtains, shower shoes and bucket, backpack, raincoat, answering machine (Steph would bring the computer), clothes, posters, more clothes (It was a good thing Dad quickly agreed to follow her to school—she needed the space in the van!), stereo. Her car—used, but still *her* car—was washed and filled with gas. Class registration information was in her notebook. Alexandra knew there was not much chance of getting all the classes she wanted, since the freshmen registered after everyone else. No matter. She would adjust. Finally she would be on her own. No more curfew. No more little brother around all the time. No more, "Don't you want one more scoop of potatoes?" at the supper table. Freedom.

A small problem had come up. On the crisp fall day when it was time to finally depart, *independence day,* Dad was being—well, he was being a Dad. In the classic Dad voice, he had said, "I will lead the way—I have several accounts in the town where we are headed, and I know the way." Maybe it wasn't such a big deal, but all of a sudden, Alex felt like a little girl again. She had wanted to drive it alone—letting Dad come later (like at night) with her clothes. Now he pulled the power trip. "You haven't ever driven it by yourself," was followed by the "directions lecture," followed by the "highlighter on the map" scene. What was he saying now about, "in case we get separated?" Puh-leeze. Let's just get on the road.

Still determined to assert her independence, but deep down knowing that Dad meant well, Alexandra allowed herself to fall behind. She could see the minivan about half a mile ahead. Thoughts of campus temporarily replaced the desire to be in charge of the journey. It was time for lunch. Alex caught up and passed the van. When she took the next exit, her father followed her down the ramp. He didn't say much when she pulled into the restaurant of her choice. After the lunch stop, the half-mile following distance grew until Alex could barely see the minivan. With two more hours in the drive, it was time to settle into some music. Alexandra looked through her CD case until she found just the right one. Her mind disappeared in the music, and when she decided to pay attention again, the van was nowhere in sight. Her mind raced. At first she thought, "I will just meet up with Dad on campus." As the miles went by, she became less sure of the route. She looked at the highlighted map and realized she had gone past the exit for the state road that led to the university about twenty miles ago. However, there was another road on the map that looked just as good, and it was straight ahead. Three hours, two construction detours, and many miles later, Alexandra was really lost.

▶▶▶▶▶ ▶▶▶▶▶▶▶▶▶▶▶▶▶▶▶

▲ Chat Room ▲▲▲▲▲▲▲▲▲▲▲▲▲▲▲

Rank the problems Alexandra had from 1 to 10, with 1 being the "fatal flaw" and 10 being, "She's just being herself." Defend your answers, either to your group or on the website (if you are doing this individually).

____ blinded by her own ego
____ didn't study the map
____ lack of respect for her father
____ took too much stuff to college and needed two vehicles
____ didn't pay attention to the "if we get separated" plan
____ control freak
____ college was too far away
____ state highway department should have fixed the road
____ Dad should have recognized her need to be the leader
____ other (you identify it)

Was Alexandra aware of her need to follow Dad? Jot down what you think.

Describe briefly in the space below a time when you thought you knew the way and resisted the opportunity to follow a leader or heed advice, and then discovered that you really should have listened after all.

What spiritual application can you make from the case study?

▲▲▲▲▲▲▲▲▲▲▲▲▲▲▲▲▲▲▲▲▲▲▲

THE NEED TO FOLLOW PRINCIPLE

I am a big fan of James Bond and spy movies with thriller stuff where you don't know who did it until the end of the movie. Spy gadgets like Q invents for 007 and which McGyver made from household items, are particularly fun. These shows are also educational. Here is a sampling of things I have learned from these movies:[1]

△ At least one of a pair of identical twins is born evil.

△ When defusing a bomb, don't worry which wire to cut. You will sweat a lot, but you will always choose the right one.

△ Most laptop computers are powerful enough to override the communications system of an enemy government.

▶▶▶▶▶▶▶▶▶▶▶▶▶▶▶▶▶▶▶▶▶▶▶

Δ It does not matter if you are heavily outnumbered in a fight involving martial arts—your enemies will wait patiently to attack you one by one by dancing around in a threatening manner until you have knocked out their predecessors.

Δ If you are blonde and pretty, it is possible to become a world expert on nuclear fission at the age of 22.

Δ Rather than wasting bullets, megalomaniacs prefer to kill their archenemies using complicated machinery involving fuses, pulley systems, deadly gasses, lasers, and man-eating sharks, which will allow their captives at least 20 minutes to escape.

Δ The ventilation system of any building is the perfect hiding place. No one will ever think of looking for you in there, and you can travel to any other part of the building you want without difficulty.

Δ A man will show no pain while taking the most ferocious beating, but will wince when a woman tries to clean his wounds.

One other thing I have learned is that spies always operate on a "need to know" basis. They work on limited information until they have already taken off on the crowded airplane, about to start a mission. The tape (that will eventually self-destruct) will be taped to the airline seat. Then nobody notices the acid smell or the smoke when the tape has a meltdown.

Jesus' followers operated on a "need to follow" basis. When they signed up, it is doubtful they understood that they would be going out and preaching and driving out demons. Jesus knew they didn't need to know that—yet.

Jesus went up on a mountainside and called to him those he wanted, and they came to him. He appointed twelve—designating them apostles—that they might be with him and that he might send them out to preach and to have authority to drive out demons. These are the twelve he appointed: Simon (to whom he gave the name Peter); James son of Zebedee and his brother John (to them he gave the name Boanerges, which means Sons of Thunder); Andrew, Philip, Bartholomew, Matthew, Thomas, James son of Alphaeus, Thaddaeus, Simon the Zealot and Judas Iscariot, who betrayed him (Mark 3:13-19).

▲Chat Room▲ ▲ ▲ ▲ ▲ ▲ ▲ ▲ ▲ ▲ ▲ ▲

Make a list of the twelve disciples. Before you look back at the passage printed above, see how many names you can get from memory. After each name, write out what you know about them—occupation, family, physical appearance, personality . . .

1._____   7._____

2._____   8._____

3._____   9._____

4._____ 10._____

5._____ 11._____

6._____ 12._____

Pick a factor you believe one of the twelve weighed as he considered Jesus' invitation to follow Him.

For further information, consult a good Bible dictionary for articles on each of the twelve. Bonus points if you find the thirteenth—the one Jesus didn't call at all.

▲▲▲▲▲▲▲▲▲▲▲▲▲▲▲▲▲▲▲

Twelve Ordinary People

Each of the twelve was a person Jesus called as a follower. They were *those He wanted* (emphasis mine). Who were they? Religious super-stars with Bible drill trophies lining their shelves? Hardly. Peter, Andrew, James, and John were fishermen, possibly all from the same town (Bethsaida according to the first chapter of John's Gospel). Peter was the recognized leader of the disciples, and we know more about him than the others. Andrew was the behind-the-scenes outreach guy. He was responsible for introducing Peter, Philip, and Bartholomew to Jesus. Matthew was a tax collector. His name means "gift of God" though through his occupation, he enjoyed the "gifts of others." Just kidding.

Thomas was the one remembered for his doubting, though I am not convinced that history has given him a fair shake. John 20:19 says the disciples were behind locked doors because of fear. Thomas wasn't with them. Maybe he wasn't afraid. Simon was a zealot (political activist), and Judas was the betrayer. We don't know much about the others, and there is even some question about who is whom according to slight dif-ferences in the lists of apostles given by Matthew and John.

So much for the biographies. A more important question here is: *Why* did they follow Jesus? Nothing is recorded in the Bible about motiva-tion, but that is where followology comes in. The principle says we are motivated by our need. If we need to go somewhere and someone knows the way, we are motivated to follow. Each of the twelve who responded to Jesus' invitation to follow was motivated by something missing in his life. Once the disciples started following Jesus, following became their job description. They rarely knew where He was going— but when Jesus got up and left, they followed.

▶▶▶▶▶▶▶▶▶▶▶▶▶▶▶▶▶▶▶▶▶▶

If You Don't Know the Way, You Should Follow the Leader

Disciples operate on a "need to follow" basis. Our motivation for following is always in direct proportion to our awareness of our need. If we are convinced of the way, we will not be interested in following. Ego-blind people do not make good followers. A spy who disregards instructions on tape does not live to make a sequel to the movie.

CHRISTLIKE RELATIONSHIPS

I began following Christ because my sister Carol didn't want to get on the bus alone. She started going to a small church in Richardson, Texas, because a girl who was in the band with her was the pastor's daughter. The church sent a school bus through neighborhoods to pick up people for church, and my sister talked me into following her. I can't honestly say what my need was then. I do not remember what motivated me to listen to the preacher talk about Jesus for the first time. Even when I was baptized, I was not aware of what it meant to follow Him. In the early days of my Christianity, I was ignorant of the cost of discipleship. Like the disciples, what was ahead would have scared me. *I was, however, willing to learn what it meant to have the God of the universe slowly begin to reshape my life.*

See if you can find yourself in the biblical descriptions of several men who were challenged to follow Jesus:

As they were walking along the road, a man said to him, "I will follow you wherever you go." Jesus replied, "Foxes have holes and birds of the air have nests, but the Son of Man has no place to lay his head." He said to another man, "Follow me." But the man replied, "Lord, first let me go and bury my father." Jesus said to him, "Let the dead bury their own dead, but you go and proclaim the kingdom of God." Still another said, "I will follow you, Lord; but first let me go back and say good-by to my family." Jesus replied, "No one who puts his hand to the plow and looks back is fit for service in the kingdom of God (Luke 9:57-62).

▲Chat Room▲▲▲▲▲▲▲▲▲▲▲▲▲▲

According to the dialogue with Jesus, what do you believe was the primary motivation for each of the three men in the passage?

Person 1—

Person 2—

Person 3—

Name a barrier that potentially kept them from becoming followers.

Person 1—

Person 2—

Person 3—

▲▲▲▲▲▲▲▲▲▲▲▲▲▲▲▲▲▲▲

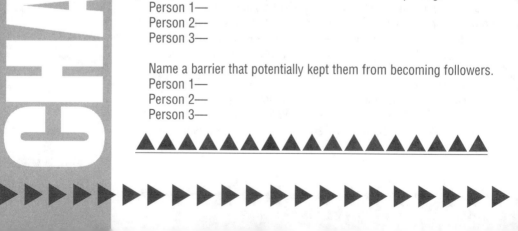

THE ROLE CONFUSION BARRIER

I remember one of my favorite "parent stories" (the ones that embarrass the children involved and mainly amuse other adults) regarding my son, Aaron. He was playing with an older child in the church nursery when he decided he had enough of being a follower. He pulled away from the other child and said, "You're not the boss of me!" As he has become a pre-teenager, Aaron has not come right out and said that I wasn't his boss, but his body language and his rolled eyes tell me that inside his head, he occasionally looks at Dad and says, "You're not the boss of me!" Role confusion is not confined to friend-to-friend and Dad-to-son relationships. Similar tensions can exist between leaders and followers.

In the movie *Big*, a little boy wanted to be a grown-up. He got his wish, but he was really just a child in an adult body (Tom Hanks played the role). He ended up with a dream job—trying out toys. The idea behind the whole movie was how ludicrous it is to try to trade identities (roles) with someone else. You can probably think of movies or stories that follow the same theme.

▲Chat Room▲▲▲▲▲▲▲▲▲▲▲▲▲▲

Name a movie or story that features the theme of a person who traded identities with someone else (i.e. *Face Off, The Parent Trap*). Now it is your turn.

What had to change about the relationship between the two people who traded identities? Choose all which apply. They had to. . .
- ❏ become like the other person
- ❏ dress like the other person
- ❏ talk like the other person
- ❏ switch schools
- ❏ assume the emotional nature
- ❏ tell mom who was whom
- ❏ smell like the other person
- ❏ take other person's boyfriend/girlfriend

Consider some follower/leader relationships. Among your group, or online, suggest an answer to each of the following:[2]
- • What does a conductor want from musicians?
- • What does a teacher want from students?
- • What does a boss want from employees?
- • What does a coach want from players?
- • What does a parent want from children?
- • What does a general want from soldiers?
- • What does a ruler want from citizens?

▲▲▲▲▲▲▲▲▲▲▲▲▲▲▲▲▲▲▲▲

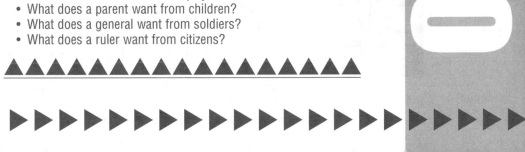

CHAPTER TWO

Ask committed Christians if they understand that Jesus is the leader instead of them, and they will give you an odd look and say, "Well, of course, Jesus is the leader." Yet, if we believe this, why do we live as if we're in charge of our lives so much of the time? The root problem may be role confusion. It is vital for a disciple to come to grips with the fact that in the relationship with Jesus as our leader, He is "the boss of me."

We can learn from the first disciples that it is difficult to play follow the leader. We follow until we think we are getting the hang of it, and then we say, "Thanks, Jesus, but I'll take it from here." This cannot be. We are called to be living sacrifices (Rom. 12:1-2), though someone has reminded us that the problem with living sacrifices is that they keep rolling off the altar.

Check out a day in the life of Jesus and the disciples. Look up Mark 1:35-37 and compare the expectations Jesus had for the day with the expectations the disciples had. In Capernaum, Jesus had been doing the things of ministry—healing, casting out demons, teaching. Exciting stuff.

Decision Time

Where were the disciples? They looked for Jesus but couldn't find Him. He had an agenda that wasn't the same as theirs. They had agreed to follow Jesus, but they had certain expectations about what that experience would entail. They figured their expectations were on target, considering all they had given up to follow Jesus. But it seemed like they were ready to take it from here. They had gotten the hang of the teaching, healing, casting out thing, and if Jesus would just—well, if He would just follow. But He wouldn't. He was off praying when the crowds were gathered for the exciting stuff. Instead of going toward the crowds, Jesus took off in the other direction. The disciples faced a decision as to whether they would continue to follow or try to take off on their own.

The followology principle is tested against the barrier of role confusion. Go back to the first of this chapter and remind yourself of the first followology principle. Write it out here:

Followology Principle:

_____

_____

A disciple is motivated by the need to follow the leader. When we forget what it was like before we started following Jesus, the need to have

> "Like , I *know* how to drive, okay?"

Him in front showing the way may seem to diminish. It is easy to repress the empty feeling we had before. When our awareness of the need to follow lessens, we are less motivated to continue following. Do you remember when you learned how to drive? At first (hopefully), you were ready to receive instruction from a driver's ed instructor, or someone else experienced in the art of vehicular navigation (er, driving). As you drove more, you gained confidence. If your instructor continued to sit beside you and constantly give instructions, you would probably respond, *"Like, I* know *how to drive, okay?"*

Confidence is good, but if you stop taking hints from someone further down the road (pardon the pun), then your overconfidence results in role reversal, and often in a wreck. Statistically, youth and young adults are most likely to have automobile accidents. Usually the accident results from excessive speed in conditions that do not permit it. Wisdom gained with experience prevents many such accidents.

Consider one final scenario here. What if your driver's ed instructor were Richard Petty or some other famous racecar driver? When someone who has driven a car over 200 miles-per-hour says you are going too fast, would it make a difference? Probably. The difference is that you have, or at least you should have, tremendous respect for someone who is an expert in his or her field. How much more is Jesus an expert in followology? He knows better than we do how our lives need to unfold. Only when we try to change places with our Leader do we forget what motivated us to follow Him in the first place.

Role confusion causes us to forget how much we need to follow Jesus. The result is that we miscalculate our ability to control our lives. We feel self-sufficient, confident, and cocky. And usually we crash. Addiction, eating disorders, and other excessive behaviors are signs that young adults are trying to shout, "I am in control." But self-sufficiency is a lie. In our innermost quiet places, we know that we do not know the way. But Jesus does. In John 15:5, Jesus reminded us that, "apart from me you can do nothing."

▲Chat Room▲ ▲ ▲ ▲ ▲ ▲ ▲ ▲ ▲ ▲ ▲ ▲

Write out the following statement: "Jesus is the leader; I am the follower. My goal today is to follow His schedule, accomplish His agenda, reach His destination, and love those He sends my way." Write it in the space below. It's almost like homework!!!

Name one way your life would change if that statement became the prayer and goal of your heart every day.

When Jesus' agenda becomes your agenda, how will that affect your motivation to follow Him?

▲▲▲▲▲▲▲▲▲▲▲▲▲▲▲▲▲▲▲ ▲

Let's review, even though there is no final exam. If need determines the motivation for following, it is reasonable to assume that we will not follow Jesus unless we see a need. I once heard a story about a would-

CROSS SEEKERS

be follower who was led by his teacher to the bank of a small stream. The teacher suspected the student was following him without much commitment. The two knelt beside the creek to talk about the direction their time together would go. As they talked about the commitment it would take to proceed with the lessons, the teacher suddenly grabbed the student by the hair and plunged his head under water. After what seemed like a long time, the teacher pulled the student out of the water. Gasping for air, the student started to say something to his teacher, but the teacher thrust his head back under the water, this time for a few seconds longer. When the teacher finally allowed the student to come out of the water again, the student gulped oxygen, then began to protest. The teacher responded, "When you want to learn from me as badly as you wanted that next breath, then you will be ready to follow me."

Role confusion can be a barrier to seeing the need. If the student merely wanted the teacher to get him started, then he needed a librarian more than he needed a teacher. We are the followers, and Jesus is the teacher. Our continued perspective on that relationship is a key to our motivation to follow.

As disciples, we should ask God every day to remind us how silly it is for us to think we are the leaders. Being a follower is an awesome role. Live every day with that profound truth in your mind, and you will take a giant step in earning your degree in followology. Along the way, you become a better follower of Jesus.

In spite of the difficulties involved with making sure we are committed to our role as followers, and with keeping our motivation for following as the need we have for Jesus, let's move on. The next chapter looks at the second principle of followology, the principle of choice. You will also consider how spiritual pride can stand in the way of making this principle effective in your journey as a followologist.

Notes
1. Adapted from an email that was sent around by some of my strange friends.
2. Martin R. De Haan II, *What Does It Take To Follow Christ?* (Grand Rapids, MI: RBC Ministries, 1992), 4.

ARE YOU STILL FOLLOWING?

C H A P T E R   T H R E E

FOLLOWING BY CHOICE WITH PRIDE ASIDE

Followology Principle: *The Choice Principle describes our responsibility to follow.*
Followology Barrier: *Spiritual Pride (Followers acknowledge that they need their leaders.)*

The only word Tim could think of to describe his feelings at the moment was "awesome." He had been offered a bid in a fraternity on campus, the one that guys really wanted to get in. All of a sudden, he felt a rush of pride that he had been judged worthy to be a Kappa

CHAPTER THREE

Sigma. In his heart, he knew that a frat was a frat, but some guys from the Kappa Sig house were in his business law class and a conversational friendship in class led to a bid during rush week.

Tim was a sophomore. When he came to the university, he was terrified that his grades would fall and he would lose the scholarship that his high school grades had earned him. Tim had a deal with his dad. Dad agreed to pay tuition, room, and board. All other expenses were up to Tim. He got an off-campus job that paid pretty well, and it didn't require so much time that he couldn't study. So he worked at his part time job, he went to church on Sunday morning and Sunday night—they fed college students for free at the local church on Sunday nights—and he studied. And he studied. And he studied.

The liberal arts core that he took as a freshman was challenging. College Algebra 101 was everything it was supposed to be (grad student trying to make a reputation!). For degree of difficulty, Tim figured it to be about a seven. English Composition seemed like nonsense ("Write an essay speculating as to the personality of a banana . . ."). Philosophy class allowed him to explore "Existentialism from Dostoevsky to Sartre." His Western Civilization class was taught by an ex-army colonel who seemed to subtitle the course, "Christianity 101 meets Humanism 102." In tenth grade, Tim had become a Christian. He had been involved in church back home—youth group was where he had been introduced to the term "disciple" and had started having quiet times and even memorizing some Scripture. As a freshman, it seemed like everything he believed in was being challenged, but he survived with his faith intact and growing and his name on the dean's list.

In the fall of his second year at school, he knew that he could cut it academically. As he looked back at his freshman year, he had a feeling he had missed out on some things. Work, church, and the library were the only places he ever went. The fellowship at church was fine, but he could name the close friends he had made by counting 20% of the fingers on one hand. Tim wanted to be involved with something on campus, something that would allow him to meet some people. He went to meetings held by some of the Christian groups, and it was a good experience. Now he was faced with another choice. A fraternity wanted him to pledge.

One morning, though, his quiet time guide asked the question, "How many non-Christians do you know?" Tim had to admit that he only knew a few names of people in some of his classes. He sensed that God wanted him to reach out more. Was the fraternity a chance to follow God in this, or would it turn out like some of his friends warned that it would? When he got his bid, he got advice from some of his friends. Most of them warned him that the frat was a terrible choice and that he would be a hard core alcoholic in no time.

One choice was safe. Tim could continue to work, study, go to church, and occasionally attend a Christian meeting on campus. The other choice held the possibility that he could do something for God or that he could mess up royally. One choice would be seen by some of his church friends as "resisting temptation" while the other choice had uncertainty. Tim decided to accept the bid and become a Kappa Sigma pledge.

▲Chat Room▲ ▲ ▲ ▲ ▲ ▲ ▲ ▲ ▲ ▲ ▲ ▲ ▲

What would you have advised Tim to do? Why?

Tim tried to write out all of the choices along with the potential con- sequences. The napkin he was writing on is reproduced for you below. List the possible outcomes associated with each choice.

⚙ **PIZZA TIME**

If I choose to join the fraternity:

If I choose to stay in the dorm as an independent:

CHAPTER THREE

True Confessions

I have a confession to make. The person whom I called "Tim" in the case study was really me. I no longer have the napkin that I wrote on, but I did have to make the choice. I knew that I had only been a Christian for a few years, and that I had grown up in a home where alcohol was present. I didn't know how strong I would be, and I could easily follow the wrong crowd (or leader). I did know that the guys in the frat house were an interesting group of guys. And I did choose to pledge Kappa Sigma. I didn't become an alcoholic, and I was able to begin some Bible study groups in the house. Several of my fellow frat boys came to know Jesus. They even elected me as the pledge trainer. I feel like I made the right choice—that God helped me to follow Jesus in the context of the Greek system. However, I confess that I did have a bit of pride in that they chose me to be part of their group. A little later in this chapter, you and I will explore together as to how such pride can be an obstacle to following Jesus.

WITNESS

Following a Wrong Leader—With Tragic Results

While I had a positive experience, I do not endorse the fraternity for everyone. Sometimes following a Greek organization has negative results. I read in the New Orleans paper of a real life story of a young man who followed the wrong leader as he chose to party with his fraternity friends. I downloaded this story from the net:[1]

Mike Turner knows what it is like to drink with the "Three Wise Men." With a mixture of Bacardi 151-proof rum, Goldschlager and Jagermeister, the potent "Three Wise Men" drink is guaranteed to get anyone drunk—really drunk.

"I usually have to stop at three drinks in about two hours," Turner said. "I get to the point where I can't focus anymore and I have to stop, but I never think about whether or not I am approaching a toxic level."

A Louisiana State University pledge did reach a toxic level less than one month ago.

It was a variation of this powerful, trendy mixture which helped kill Benjamin Wynne at his fraternity house on Aug. 26.

Wynne's blood alcohol level was widely reported at .588, soaring almost six times over the level at which most state laws consider a person legally intoxicated. Authorities said the autopsy found Wynne had consumed the equivalent of 24 drinks that night.

The alcohol poisoning death of Wynne after his bid-acceptance party at the LSU Sigma Alpha Epsilon house has once again placed the spotlight on fraternities and binge drinking.

When asked about the LSU tragedy, SWT Interfraternity Council Advisor Rob Lydic said the fraternity lacked responsibility, and Wynne lacked the education that should come when drinking alcohol.

Lydic said alcohol is accessible for college students no matter where they are. Whether in a bar on the Square, on a dance floor in an Austin club, in a private residence or in a fraternity house, binge drinking is common.

Benjamin Wynne and his friends chose the leader that they would follow. They made the wrong choice. That leader was not Jesus. The comment by the IFC advisor underscores that the responsibility for the choice to "follow the alcoholic leader" was made by the students. I do not agree that they lacked education. Even college freshmen are intelligent, thinking adults. Some young adults are driven by a need to be accepted, a need to fit in, a need to. . .well, you fill in the blanks. Choices are made based on what needs we think we have, and there are always consequences that occur as a result of those choices. The problem comes when we are either too proud to stand on our own convictions, or we get caught up in the emotion of following.

THE CHOICE PRINCIPLE

In Followology, the process unfolds the same way. The Need Principle describes the motivation for following. The Choice Principle focuses on the responsibility for following. If need convinces us that we do not know the way, a choice must be made, a choice for which we will be held responsible. Don't miss this:

A defining moment occurs. Before the choice, you are not following. After the choice, you are following.

A defining moment is one that causes everyone to stop and change direction. Almost every generation in our country's history has had a defining moment. Baby Boomers had the assassination of President John F. Kennedy. Baby Busters had the explosion of the space shuttle *Challenger*. Perhaps the deaths of Princess Diana and Mother Teresa in the same week were collectively a defining moment for another generation. When an event like the ones mentioned occurs, we remember precisely where we were when we heard the news. For the disciples, the call to follow Jesus was such an event.

No, Really, Jesus—We're Coming!

The twelve disciples are an intriguing lot to study. Though Jesus challenged them to leave what they were doing and follow Him, their commitment was progressively greater. In the last chapter, you were introduced to all twelve by name. I talked to a New Testament professor here at the seminary. He said that we should understand that there is a greater emphasis placed on the disciples collectively than individually. In other words, by this time the disciples we listed in Chapter 2

> *A defining moment occurs. Before the choice, you are not following. After the choice, you are following.*

were widely known as "the twelve."

As Jesus' ministry continued, the crowd of real disciples got smaller. The commitment level of the apostles and others who stuck with Jesus increased even as the numbers decreased. At least some of the ones who were called disciples later dropped out of the pack. In Matthew's account of the calling of the disciples, the word "disciple" is used to describe one of the would-be followers who professed a desire to go with Jesus, but who apparently did not stay with it. Compare the use of the word "disciple" in the following verses. See if you can see a progressive commitment:

Matthew 5:1
Matthew 8:23
Matthew 8:25
Matthew 9:10
Matthew 9:11
Matthew 9:14
Matthew 9:19
Matthew 9:37

Matthew 10:1: "He called his twelve disciples to him and gave them authority to drive out evil spirits and to heal every disease and sickness."

I included the last verse because I was afraid you would get lazy. All the way in chapter 10 of Matthew's account of Jesus' life, the Bible says that Jesus finally had the twelve designated apostles together. Look at Luke 6:13: "When morning came, he called his disciples to him and chose twelve of them, whom he also designated apostles."

WITNESS

The difference in "disciple" and "apostle" is significant. There was a larger group of disciples who followed Jesus (possibly hundreds at first) and from which Jesus called the twelve. In Greek, the word for apostle is *apostolos* (ap-OS-tol-os) which indicates a delegate or an ambassador. An apostle is commissioned or ordained (see Mark 3:13 in the *King James Version*). The apostles were sent out on a mission trip (Matt. 10) and instructed to cast out demons and heal people who were sick. In addition, they were to proclaim the kingdom of heaven (Matt. 10:7). With the responsibility of being an apostle came the ability to do miracles to testify to the validity of Jesus' ministry.

▲Chat Room▲▲▲▲▲▲▲▲▲▲▲▲▲

If possible, pinpoint a "defining moment" when you made a choice that radically changed the course of your life. Have you thought of it? Now hold it!

If Jesus challenged you to follow Him today (no kidding, if He challenged you), would you be a disciple or an apostle? Jot down two reasons why.

▶▶▶▶▶   ▶▶▶▶▶▶▶▶▶▶▶▶▶▶▶

1.

2.

▲▲▲▲▲▲▲▲▲▲▲▲▲▲▲▲▲▲▲▲▲

Back to Our Metaphor

Let's lighten up a little and go back to our physical following metaphor. Have you ever followed someone you *thought* was the right leader? You understood that you had a need. You probably correctly identified the need. You chose to follow, believing that the need would be met. Even as you followed, you were convinced that the person in front of you was the right leader. I see two things at work here. First, our wrong choice may be a case of mistaken identity. As a youth minister, I remember leaving a youth conference at a coliseum. I was behind another rental van, driven by an adult who said, "Allen, I know a great place for us to take the group to eat. Just follow me." I still have this picture of looking down at something—probably something that had just been thrown at me—and looking back up to see the reassuring sight of the rental van that I would follow to nourishment.

One problem that I did not think about then, but yea, verily, I see quite clearly now. *All rental vans that were ever made look like all other rental vans that were ever made.* This is not found in the real Bible, but in the "Handbook of Things People Who Take Trips in Groups Should Know." I followed the white van all the way to Wendy's. I was beginning to wonder what was so special about Wendy's as a place to eat when I saw the youth pressing their noses against the glass in the back of the van ahead. I didn't recognize any of them. I had followed the wrong van to the wrong restaurant. I had chosen the wrong leader. The price of the wrong choice was separation from my group.

> All rental vans that were ever made look like all other rental vans that were ever made.

Higher prices have been paid for the wrong choice of a leader. On April 19, 1993, 72 men, women and children died because the Branch Davidians cult in Waco, Texas followed David Koresh.[2] On October 1, 1946, an international jury pronounced guilty verdicts for the leaders of Germany's Third Reich. They had followed Adolf Hitler and their wrong choice of a leader led to execution by hanging on October 16 of the same year. The price is high when people follow the wrong leader.[3]

As a college student, many voices scream at you to follow them. Your choice to follow should be based on an honest assessment of your physical, emotional, social, intellectual, and spiritual needs. Once the initial choice is made to follow, everything is changed. Before I pledged the fraternity, I was not a member. When I joined, I changed my place of residence, I made some new friends, I became affiliated with a group for a lifetime. Before I decided to follow the "imposter van" to Wendy's, I was a part of a group, but my choice to follow the wrong van placed me with a different group. When our choices are informed and prayerfully weighed, we have a better shot at success, but regardless of the outcome, we are responsible for the choice of leaders that we follow.

As a followologist and student minister, it seems natural to me that the twelve struggled with some of the early days of discipleship with Jesus. Yes, there was an initial decision to follow Him, but the decision came after He had achieved some popularity. We cannot miss, however, that at the crucial moment, the disciples made their choice, left everything, and followed Him. Years later when the crowds deserted Him, the midterm exam would be given.

> From this time many of his disciples turned back and no longer followed him. "You do not want to leave too, do you?" Jesus asked the Twelve. Simon Peter answered him, "Lord, to whom shall we go? You have the words of eternal life. We believe and know that you are the Holy One of God" (John 6:66-69).

AND NOW LADIES AND GENTLEMEN, ON CENTER STAGE . . . SPIRITUAL PRIDE!

As I finished typing the heading to this paragraph, I could hear the announcer shouting, "Give it up for spiritual pride . . ." Spiritual pride stands as an obstacle to choosing the right spiritual leader to follow. I love an old joke that involves the dreaded pride issue. It goes something like this:

> A U.S. Naval destroyer was sailing the seas with the crew looking forward to being in port soon. A dense fog had rolled in, making visibility almost impossible. On the bridge of the ship, a call came over the ship's radio: "Attention. You are on a collision course. Please bear 20 degrees to the starboard side."
>
> The captain of the ship, like his crew, was tired from their long voyage, and he just happened to be on the bridge at the time. The voice didn't sound very official to him, so he took the microphone himself. He said, "This is a United States naval vessel. I urge you, sir, bear 20 degrees to your starboard."
>
> The other voice replied, "Negative sir. Urge you to bear 20 degrees starboard."
>
> The captain, now growing a bit testy, shot back, "I am the captain in the United States Navy. Urge that you bear 20 degrees starboard."
>
> The voice replied, "Negative, Sir. I am an ensign first class and I urge that you bear 20 degrees starboard."
>
> The captain was getting angry. He couldn't believe an ensign would refuse his order. "Negative, ensign. I command a naval warship. I have nuclear weaponry aboard. I order you to bear 20 degrees starboard."

CHAPTER THREE

The voice came back. "Negative, Captain. I have no weaponry aboard. Nevertheless, I urge that you bear 20 degrees starboard."

Now furious, the captain decided he would get to the bottom of this subordination. "Ensign, I command that you let me speak to your commanding officer. You are refusing a direct order. I am ordering you to bear 20 degrees starboard."

The voice replied one last time. "Negative Sir. I urge you to bear 20 degrees to your starboard and I have no commanding officer here. *I am the lighthouse.*

Pride is different from role confusion. There would be no doubt under normal circumstances that the captain outranked the ensign. However, given the weather conditions, the captain should have been motivated by his need for direction. He should have chosen to be open to instruction. Had he known from the beginning that the lowly ensign was commanding the lighthouse, things might have been different. But, as the joke goes, they weren't.

Spiritual pride can be similar. Jesus' disciples (the twelve) help us to see this clearly. They accidentally stumbled on a major barrier to our being better followers of Jesus. The disciples often argued about who was or would be the greatest disciple when the kingdom of God finally arrived. They had a bit of a misconception as to what the kingdom actually was. They thought it was an earthly thing, with princes and dukes and knights and such. They pictured an established pecking order. So they argued about who would outrank whom on the basis of how spiritual they were.

▲ Chat Room (actually a little Bible Study) ▲ ▲ ▲ ▲

In the following passages, take a highlighter and highlight the phrases that indicate spiritual pride among the disciples:

Now as Jesus was going up to Jerusalem, he took the twelve disciples aside and said to them, "We are going up to Jerusalem, and the Son of Man will be betrayed to the chief priests and the teachers of the law. They will condemn him to death and will turn him over to the Gentiles to be mocked and flogged and crucified. On the third day he will be raised to life!" Then the mother of Zebedee's sons came to Jesus with her sons and, kneeling down, asked a favor of him. "What is it you want?" he asked. She said, "Grant that one of these two sons of mine may sit at your right and the other at your left in your kingdom." "You don't know what you are asking," Jesus said to them. "Can you drink the cup I am going to drink?" "We can," they answered. Jesus said to them, "You will indeed drink from my cup, but to sit at my right or left is not for me to grant. These places belong to those for whom they have been prepared by my Father." When the ten heard about this, they were indignant with the two brothers. Jesus called them together and said, "You know that the rulers of the Gentiles lord it

over them, and their high officials exercise authority over them. Not so with you. Instead, whoever wants to become great among you must be your servant, and whoever wants to be first must be your slave—just as the Son of Man did not come to be served, but to serve, and to give his life as a ransom for many" (Matt. 20:17-28).

Also a dispute arose among them as to which of them was considered to be greatest. Jesus said to them, "The kings of the Gentiles lord it over them; and those who exercise authority over them call themselves Benefactors. But you are not to be like that. Instead, the greatest among you should be like the youngest, and the one who rules like the one who serves. For who is greater, the one who is at the table or the one who serves? Is it not the one who is at the table? But I am among you as one who serves" (Luke 22:24-27).

Go back and look at what you highlighted. Think about why you highlighted it. Can you identify this in your spiritual walk?

❏ Yes   ❏ No   ❏ Maybe

▲▲▲▲▲▲▲▲▲▲▲▲▲▲▲▲▲▲▲▲▲

In each case, the disciples heard the lesson but missed the point. The issue didn't die there. It came up several other times. In each case, the twelve knew that Jesus was the leader, but their pride rose up to the point of discontent with that relationship. Even at the last supper, after Jesus had shown true humility by washing His disciples' feet, they didn't get it. In Luke 22:33, Simon Peter responded to Jesus' prediction that he (Peter) would falter with a resounding reply: "'Lord, I am ready to go with you to prison and to death.'" Matthew's account is less flattering to Peter. In Matthew 26:33, Peter replied, "'Even if all fall away on account of you, I never will.'" Not only did Peter reveal his own pride, he did so at the expense of the other disciples. The leader responded with what must have been a chilling reply: Jesus answered, "'I tell you, Peter, before the rooster crows today, you will deny three times that you know me'" (Luke 22:35).

A complete contrast to spiritual pride is found in the example of John the Baptist. While in prison, he sought to know if his cousin was the Messiah. When he received reports of what Jesus was doing, he stated, "'A man can receive only what is given him from heaven. You yourselves can testify that I said, "I am not the Christ but am sent ahead of him." . . . He must become greater; I must become less'" (John 3:27-28,30).

As followologists, how do we avoid the barrier of spiritual pride? Why not imitate John? Our goal should be for Jesus to increase through all we do, all we say, and all we think. With this goal in place, we can pray daily that the goal is realized in all of the situations and relationships of that day.

▲Chat Room▲▲▲▲▲▲▲▲▲▲▲▲▲▲

As a Christian, define greatness based on what you have read.

Circle the situation where you are most inclined to have an attitude of spiritual pride:

(a) When I am with the Christian group on campus

(b) When I am back at my home church, hanging out with the youth group

(c) When I am asked to be in charge of something

(d) When I am at home with my family

▲▲▲▲▲▲▲▲▲▲▲▲▲▲▲▲▲▲▲▲▲▲

Laying Pride Aside Is a Daily Choice

Now you are ready to move on to another principle and another obstacle. You have decided to follow Jesus. No turning back. Your pride is behind you, and the servant leadership of Christ is before you. No turning back. You understand that you need Jesus as your leader and that you have chosen to follow Him. You may still struggle with role reversal and (like many of us) you pray daily in your battle against spiritual pride. Now you have to pay attention to the Leader and appreciate your uniqueness in the body of Christ.

Notes

1. Shannon Gilroy, "The Drinking Binge: Fraternities Climb into Spotlight with Recent LSU Overdose," *The Daily University Star ONLINE News* (URL:http://www.star.so.swt.edu/97/09/12/091297n1.html); accessed January 21, 1998.

2. Information on Branch Davidians gleaned from website, http://rampages.onramp.net/; accessed January 26, 1998.

3. Information on Hitler's men based on the article by Terrence Petty, "Hitler's Men: Judgment at Nuremberg," *The Tennessean*, 19 November 1995, cited in John Kramp, *Getting Ahead by Staying Behind*, 34.

CHAPTER THREE

▶▶▶▶▶▶▶▶▶▶▶▶▶▶▶▶▶▶▶▶▶▶

CHAPTER THREE

KEEP ON FOLLOWING!

C H A P T E R   F O U R

FOLLOWING AS LEARNER AMONG LEARNERS

Followology Principle: *The Focus Principle explains the basic discipline of following.*
Followology Barrier: *Comparison Shopping (People follow in different ways.)*

Steven saw himself as a mountain man. He wasn't like the fake out-doors types on the beer commercials—he was really comfortable being away from pavement and buildings. He was a junior at a Christian uni-versity, and his dream was to own a camp for troubled boys. He had

volunteered for an organization that took troubled boys on adventure outings to learn about themselves and how to cope with problems. Steven expanded the vision to include ministry to the boys over an entire summer. He had seen potential delinquents mature as they experienced the great outdoors for a week, and his long-range goal was to own a camp that could help other "challenged" boys by giving them a longer-term taste of wilderness living.

Dana was a 90s kind of woman. Midway through her sophomore year, she had finally chosen a major that would allow her to study in the two areas she loved the most. The first was sports. She had played volleyball and run cross-country in high school. She still ran several miles each week and played on intramural volleyball teams. She wasn't so crazy about sports that she wanted to major in fitness or coaching, but she liked to keep in shape. Dana's second love was the outdoors. As a little girl, her family had fished, camped, and hiked fairly often. She had learned to respect and love nature.

Even though Steven wanted to own a camp someday, he understood that he would need some business skills to make it happen. He had chosen to major in business administration. It was a new program at the university, a five-year degree that resulted in a Master of Business Administration. Though the main emphasis of the degree was the MBA, his program also included a minor unrelated to business administration. The intent was that someone like Steven could learn to run a business that really interested him. His minor was recreation administration with an emphasis in outdoor education.

Dana browsed through the catalog of the university and discovered a degree called Bachelor of Science in Recreation Administration. The catalog description was enticing: "The recreation major at State College develops the knowledge, skills, and attitudes to effectively plan, administer, and/or deliver quality leisure programs." Further research revealed course titles like "Individual Fitness Activities," and "Recreational Sports Leadership." Then she spied a major within the degree called "Outdoor Education." The bulletin continued:

> Outdoor Recreation majors prepare for professional careers in a wide variety of settings and plan interdisciplinary course work to meet their personal objectives. Typical careers include:
> - Outdoor Adventure Leader
> - Community Recreation Director
> - Recreation or Family Life Minister
> - Park Ranger
> - Camp Director

That was it! Even if she wasn't exactly sure which of those jobs she would want in a couple of years, the courses looked exciting. She was determined not to pick a major simply to make money in a career. Dana truly wanted to be sensitive to God's leadership in her life.

Both Dana and Steven had registered for "HPER 325, Survey of Outdoor Recreation." While it wasn't love at first sight, they had become attracted to one another. They were compatible; they were both sincere followers of Jesus and shared a love for recreation—particularly the outdoors. They had been on several dates and had gotten along well. In addition, they had begun to attend church together.

The final project in the course was in orienteering, and it involved a field trip. More like a forest trip. Each van held 10 students who were dropped off at various points along a marked trail in a National Forest. The challenge was to use a Forest Service map, plot coordinates with a compass, and arrive at a not-yet-revealed common destination. In other words, the professor had organized the hike in such a way that the students would each hike alone, but they would all end up at the same place. The class had scouted the location on another day hike, but none of them knew this was coming.

Dana and Steven were in the same van. On the way, Steven whispered to Dana, "I have been on this trail before. I will probably just walk straight to the meeting place even without the map!" Dana thought to herself, "What a guy thing! Why do they always think they can go everywhere without following directions like everyone else?"

Now Dana was in the woods by herself. She was tempted to put the map away just so she could tell Steven she didn't need to focus on the directions, either. The voice of reason spoke more loudly, however, and she carefully studied the map and slowly but confidently followed the marked trail toward the meeting point. She hoped Steven would not already be there.

Steven, on the other hand, was lost. He looked at the map when he first got off the van to get a sense of the general direction. He then put the map away and started down a trail at a rapid pace. He would arrive long before the others—or so he thought. The scenery was incredible. God had done a good job on these woods! A shortcut or two later, he realized he had not paid very close attention to the slope markings or the switchbacks. He had lost the marked trail and now found himself in a place that wasn't even on the map.

▲Chat Room▲▲▲▲▲▲▲▲▲▲▲▲▲

Who or what were Dana and Steven supposed to be following? Circle the one you feel is most correct.
- (a) The correct trail
- (b) The map
- (c) Their professor
- (d) The one who had marked the trail

Why did you circle that one? Jot your thoughts down here.
1.
2.
3.

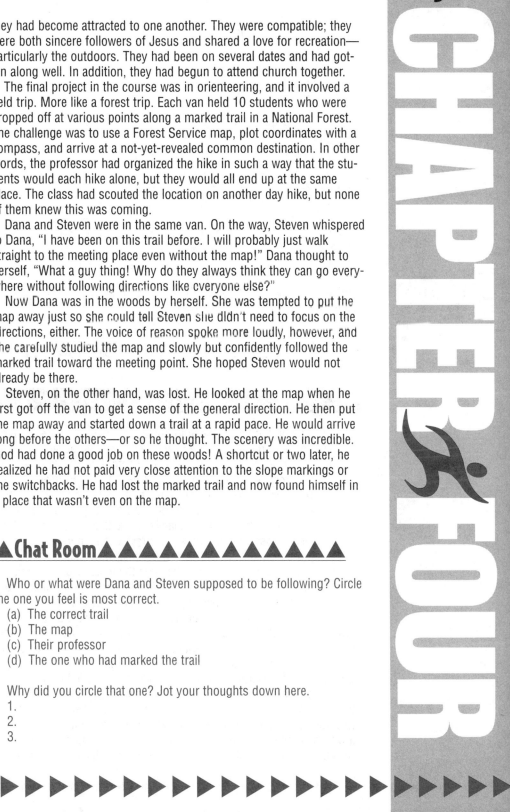

Who lost focus? Circle the one you feel is most correct.
(a) Dana
(b) Steven
(c) Both Dana and Steven
(d) None of the above

What was the main reason Steven got lost? Circle the one you feel is most correct.
(a) He refused to use the map
(b) The compass didn't work right
(c) He couldn't stop thinking about Dana
(d) He wasn't paying attention

Why do you think Steven showed up at the meeting place well behind everyone else? (Remember the barrier?)

Bonus question: What do you think the other hikers (especially Dana) said to Steven when he finally arrived?

PAY ATTENTION—FOLLOWING REQUIRES FOCUS

I hope none of that hit too close to home. As a male, it was a little too easy to write about the part where Steven assumed that because he had seen the map once and had been on the trail before, he would be able to stay focused enough to reach his destination. Followology is relatively simple if we follow the trail marked by someone who has gone before us. In the case of the disciples, it was Someone who was immediately before them—remember they were Phase One followers. Let's review one more time, using our case study. Steven was motivated by a need. He knew he needed to follow the directions on the map, given by some-one who had carefully marked the trail. He made a choice to follow the directions on the map. He got distracted by a bit of pride—but mainly, he quit paying attention. He put the map away. Dana very nearly got sidetracked by comparing herself to another follower, but she kept her focus. It was more important to follow the right trail than to be more or less of something, compared to another person.

CHRISTLIKE RELATIONSHIPS

Because you are learning the seven principles of the following process, you are now able to see spiritual implications for discipleship that others might miss. The principle of focus and the barrier of com-paring yourself to other followers are easily observed in the story that started the chapter. The Bible provides numerous passages that address both issues. Jesus was always going somewhere. Bible historians tell us

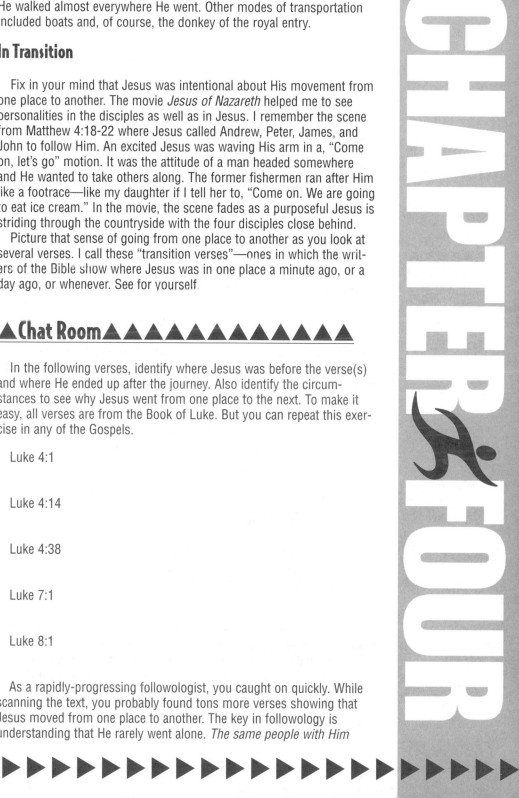

He walked almost everywhere He went. Other modes of transportation included boats and, of course, the donkey of the royal entry.

In Transition

Fix in your mind that Jesus was intentional about His movement from one place to another. The movie *Jesus of Nazareth* helped me to see personalities in the disciples as well as in Jesus. I remember the scene from Matthew 4:18-22 where Jesus called Andrew, Peter, James, and John to follow Him. An excited Jesus was waving His arm in a, "Come on, let's go" motion. It was the attitude of a man headed somewhere and He wanted to take others along. The former fishermen ran after Him like a footrace—like my daughter if I tell her to, "Come on. We are going to eat ice cream." In the movie, the scene fades as a purposeful Jesus is striding through the countryside with the four disciples close behind.

Picture that sense of going from one place to another as you look at several verses. I call these "transition verses"—ones in which the writers of the Bible show where Jesus was in one place a minute ago, or a day ago, or whenever. See for yourself.

▲Chat Room▲▲▲▲▲▲▲▲▲▲▲▲▲

In the following verses, identify where Jesus was before the verse(s) and where He ended up after the journey. Also identify the circumstances to see why Jesus went from one place to the next. To make it easy, all verses are from the Book of Luke. But you can repeat this exercise in any of the Gospels.

Luke 4:1

Luke 4:14

Luke 4:38

Luke 7:1

Luke 8:1

As a rapidly-progressing followologist, you caught on quickly. While scanning the text, you probably found tons more verses showing that Jesus moved from one place to another. The key in followology is understanding that He rarely went alone. *The same people with Him*

CHAPTER FOUR

before the transition verses were with Him after the transition verses. How does that happen? Take time to think. This one is important enough to have its own fill-in-the-blank.

How is it that the same people who were with Jesus before the transition verses were with Him afterwards as well? _____

_____

▲▲▲▲▲▲▲▲▲▲▲▲▲▲▲▲▲▲▲▲

You are absolutely correct. The disciples followed Jesus as He went from place to place. Look again at a couple of verses:

Luke 8:1: "After this, Jesus traveled about from one town and village to another, proclaiming the good news of the kingdom of God. The Twelve were with him."

Luke 22:39: "Jesus went out as usual to the Mount of Olives, and his disciples followed him."

When Jesus Went, the Disciples Followed

At the risk of one of those, Who is buried in Grant's tomb? kind of questions, How did Jesus' disciples get anywhere that He did? They followed Him. As another observer of human behavior (and possibly a fellow followologist) stated, "If no one's following, you're just taking a walk."[1] I can again picture the scene from the movie. The disciples are sitting around, talking or laughing—maybe even telling fish stories. All of a sudden, Philip or someone looks up and notices Jesus isn't there any more. He is headed for the next place. Or maybe Jesus says, "I am on my way to Jerusalem through Samaria—anyone want to come?" As the twelve lazily get to their feet, maybe it is Judas who says, "Did he say through Samaria?" And they followed.

Back to Physical Following

Move with me back into the physical metaphor. Remember the last time you were supposed to follow somebody to a destination unknown to you (like the rental van story)? Without a map or written directions, your only hope is to follow the car in front of you, driven by the one person in your group who knows the way.

Knowing that you do not know the way, you are highly motivated to follow the leader. Believing the person in the first car is going where you want to go and knows the way, you have to make a choice to follow. You recognize you cannot follow the leader if you do not focus on the leader. Motivation and commitment are at peak levels. At a red light, however, you glance over when you see that Taco Bell is having a one-night only, five soft tacos for a dollar sale, and you begin to dream about the salsa. You glance back up. The light is green, and the car in front is nowhere in sight. You didn't mean to stop following. You just got distracted.

But We Meant Well!

In spite of our best intentions to focus on our relationship with God and to allow the Holy Spirit to work in our lives, we become distracted. Remember back in Chapter 1 when we talked about following a leader you cannot see? This is the difficulty. As Phase Two followers, we can't see Jesus' back disappearing down the road and sense the physical urgency that we had better regain or we will lose sight of Him. Modern-day followers can struggle to focus on Jesus—to see what He is doing and where He is going. Following Him can be difficult, but how badly do we want to follow? As badly as the next breath of air?

Last year, my 1983 Honda went to Honda heaven. Efforts to resuscitate it proved fruitless. I was stranded in a car that would not start. A friend offered to hook a chain to my car and pull me behind his car to a repair shop. It was cheaper than a tow truck, so I agreed. Driving my Honda hooked to his van with a 20-foot length of chain, I had to pay so much attention that I had a headache by the time we got to the shop. If I was distracted for even a second, the distance between the two cars would go away in a hurry. I forced myself to pay attention.

Until we are absolutely sure we are lost without Jesus, we will not make the choice to follow Him with full focus. We must be ready to pay the price required to discipline our lives so we can see Him.

▲Chat Room▲▲▲▲▲▲▲▲▲▲▲▲▲

Name two disciplines needed to remain focused on following Jesus.

1.
2.

How can you have these disciplines in your life? Jot down 2 ideas.

1.
2.

▲▲▲▲▲▲▲▲▲▲▲▲▲▲▲▲▲▲▲▲

FOLLOWOLOGY BARRIER: COMPARISON SHOPPING

I was in charge of recreation for the retreat. As a guest, I did not know the kids very well. I decided to use two different kinds of games.

▶▶▶▶▶▶▶▶▶▶▶▶▶▶▶▶▶▶▶▶

CHAPTER FOUR

On the first afternoon, we played non-competitive games with no clear winners or losers. Until I got to know the students a little, I wanted to keep things light. We played volleyball with a sheet over the net so that nobody could spike down someone's throat. We played football with the guys on their knees to take away the element of brute force. We played trust initiative games in which the students had to achieve a goal as a team, without competing against another team. We played "Siamese soccer" with pairs of students (often intentionally mismatched) as a single player. This was achieved by tying their ankles together with bandannas, like they were in a three-legged race.

After the first day, I fully expected the kids to elect me King of Recreation and vow never to go back to games that make some feel like "losers" while others gloated in their role as "winners." Nonetheless, I had scheduled the huge everybody-in-the-camp football game for the next afternoon. During the football game, competitive juices began to flow. From the time teams were announced—I could not even imagine allowing them to choose sides—I heard cries of "not fair" and "you're gonna lose, dweeb." Even the adults who played tried a little too hard to prove their athletic prowess. (Have you ever seen deacons at a church softball game?)

At the end of the day, most of the good sportsmanship cultivated through non-competitive recreation the previous day had been unraveled. The day before, youth were working together, maximizing their individual strengths by combining them. Now many of them were trying to be something that they were not—NFL superstars. They were obsessive about everything from where to line up on a kickoff, to the number of completions required for a first down. It was a disaster!

Sometimes we treat discipleship like that ill-conceived game of football and view following Jesus as a competitive activity in which we observe other Christians and assess our performance against what they do or fail to do. While other followers can be worthy examples, and while Jesus has called all to follow, He has called us individually to follow.

Following Followers Can Be Full of Folly

> Now we look at a subtle but dangerous barrier to following Jesus—comparing ourselves to other followers.

We have studied several barriers so far. Role confusion is when we try to exchange places with Jesus, forgetting who is the Leader and who is the follower. Spiritual pride is when we become self-absorbed and seek to improve our status by being seen following Jesus. *Now we look at a subtle but dangerous barrier to following Jesus—comparing ourselves to other followers.*

In the Old Testament (Ex. 13), God instructed the Hebrews to follow the pillar of fire by night and the cloud by day. If the cloud moved, so did they. I like the mental picture that comes with the cloud or the pillar of fire. Fortunately, the cloud was tall enough to be seen over everyone's heads. If the Hebrews paid attention, they could follow God rather than other followers. How-ever, if there were a whole line of folks following the cloud, it would be tempting to simply follow the person in front of you. If a follower kept his head down, he could be led in another direction by focusing on the sandals in front of him. The problem is that when we follow others, the other person might not be following very closely, if at all. Or he might be following differently than you do. *Following any standard less than the Way, the Truth, and the Life is deadly.*

Four boys skipped school because the weather was more suitable for fishing than for learning. They all agreed that when they got back, they would tell the teacher they had a flat tire on the car. When they returned to school, they requested to take a make-up exam for a missed test. The teacher agreed and placed the boys in the four corners of the room. She told them she would read the first question, and if they all got it right, she would pass out the remainder of the exam. Then she read the first question: Which tire?

We have been talking about distractions as we try to follow Jesus. A major distraction is the temptation to compare ourselves to other fol-lowers. Though we are learners among learners, our undivided attention must be on Jesus. The first danger of comparing ourselves to other fol-lowers is the competition you thought about a few minutes ago. The second danger—illustrated with the Hebrew children a couple of para-graphs ago—is that we can settle for less than the best leader to follow.

▲ Chat Room ▲▲▲▲▲▲▲▲▲▲▲▲▲

Without writing any name down, privately ponder the following:

To whom have you compared yourself who may not be the best example?

With whom have you been competing, perhaps even sometimes spiri-tually?

▲▲▲▲▲▲▲▲▲▲▲▲▲▲▲▲▲▲▲▲▲

One Game, But Many Players

Fortunately, Jesus did not design discipleship as a competitive event in which we scout out opponents to get an edge. Jesus modeled the diversity that is the kingdom of God by choosing a mixed bag of disci-ples. The disciples varied in abilities and potential, but each was strate-gically selected for his individual strengths. Who would have picked

▶▶▶▶▶▶▶▶▶▶▶▶▶▶▶▶ ▶▶▶▶

those twelve to carry on the message of the gospel after Jesus had returned to be with the Father?

What if God assigned you the task of picking disciples?
What kind of persons would you pick?

I ran across this "something to ponder" memo. Though tongue-in-cheek, it provides perspective.[2]

Reply to: Jesus, Son of Joseph
Galilee, Israel
From: Management Consultants, Inc.

Dear Sir:

We are in receipt of the names of twelve men that you submitted for the managerial positions in your organization. We understand that you plan to retire or something within the next three years, and your intention is to leave your organization in their hands. We have reviewed your mission statement, "To Seek and Save the Lost." While we think we understand the basic nature of your work, we have some concerns about your staff.

We have run each profile through our computers, and then we conducted personal personnel (pardon the pun—kind of an inside joke around here) interviews. Each of the twelve men then had consultant visits with our staff psychologist and vocational aptitude consultant.

It is the staff's opinion that most of your nominees are lacking in background, education, and vocational aptitude for taking on the responsibility for running your organization. They are not very good team players.

Simon Peter is emotionally unstable and given to fits of temper. Andrew seems to prefer to stay in the background and lacks leadership qualities. The brothers, James and John, place personal interests above company loyalty. Thomas demonstrates a questioning attitude that would tend to undermine morale. We feel it our duty to tell you that Matthew has been blacklisted by the Jerusalem Better Business Bureau. James, the son of Alphaeus, and Thaddaeus definitely have radical leanings. They both registered a high score on the manic depression scale.

One of the candidates shows great potential. He is a man of ability and resources. He meets people well and has contacts in high places. We recommend Judas Iscariot as your comptroller and right-hand man. Forget the others.

Sincerely,

Management Consultants, Inc.

Aren't we glad that the "expert" personnel standards were not and are not used to determine the suitability for a follower of Jesus?

▲Chat Room▲ ▲ ▲ ▲ ▲ ▲ ▲ ▲ ▲ ▲ ▲ ▲ ▲

If you were a professional employment consultant, list two desirable characteristics for trainees to help Jesus with the business of followology.

1.

2.

▲▲▲▲▲▲▲▲▲▲▲▲▲▲▲▲▲▲▲▲▲▲

Ordinary Men—Extraordinary God

A quick review of the twelve produces some startling reminders. After their "fifteen minutes of fame" as they were introduced, three of them—Bartholomew, Simon (the Zealot), and James (son of Alphaeus)—are never mentioned again. Thaddaeus (also called Judas, son of James) is mentioned one more time, but that is only to clear up a case of potential mistaken identity (John 14:22). Philip and Andrew weren't in the spotlight much either. They were not in the group of disciples closest to Jesus, the "inner circle" of Peter, James, and John. But they loved and served Jesus. And Andrew was instrumental in bringing his brother Peter to Jesus (John 1:41-42), as well as the boy with the lunch when Jesus fed the 5,000 (John 6), and some Greeks who wanted to meet Jesus (John 12).

Matthew wasn't heard from much after the big party he threw when Jesus chose him as a disciple. Thomas is remembered (though maybe a bit unfairly) for doubting Jesus. Peter is recognized as having been the leader of the bunch, but was known to put his foot in his mouth often and is probably most remembered for his three denials of Jesus. James and John, the Sons of Thunder, distinguished themselves by becoming known as the two who bickered over preferential treatment in heaven. And with Judas Iscariot—well, some would say Jesus made a mistake. No one I know would name their son after him.

While all twelve stood out in their time for their potential, the Bible is honest about their glaring weaknesses. We must never forget that Jesus chose them and loved them all. Even Judas was with Jesus during His entire earthly ministry. At the last supper, Jesus continued to express love for him. As you will see in a couple of chapters, the transformation

▶ ▶

from ordinary to extraordinary happened between the Gospels and the Book of Acts. What a difference a resurrection makes!

▲Chat Room▲▲▲▲▲▲▲▲▲▲▲▲▲

Name one of Jesus' disciples most like you. Jot it down.

Which one of the twelve are you least like? Jot it down.

On the line, mark to what degree you are focused on other people rather than becoming the unique disciple that God intends for you to become.

Following other people   Following Jesus

▲▲▲▲▲▲▲▲▲▲▲▲▲▲▲▲▲▲▲▲▲▲

   My brother's testimony about how God has used him is along these lines. James is a very talented juggler and communicator. As a matter of fact, he combines juggling and speaking for some very interesting talks. When James speaks (and juggles) of his childhood and youth, he says he was in the shadow of his siblings. He is the youngest of four Jackson children, and the other three of us are good at some things. Carol is musical, Susan was a homecoming queen, and I played any sport that involved running or throwing a ball. James developed other talents since those things didn't interest him, or because he didn't feel like he was very good at them. The end of the story: I can't juggle to save my life and I have never once played sports while preaching. From my view, James got a pretty good deal. The Christian community of faith was meant to work with all followers doing what they do in their own area of strength.
   All of us bring a unique set of gifts and abilities to the table. Imagine a covered dish supper where everyone brought potato salad. Regardless of how good the potato salad was, we would wish for a little variety. In the covered dish supper that is discipleship, our diversity insures a balanced diet. Like the twelve, we must be empowered by God to follow with integrity. We, too, progress one day and make incredible mistakes the next. *Jesus never gives up on us any more than He did with the disciples.* He sees our unique potential and gives us time to develop and grow. That is why comparing our-

> **Jesus never gives up on us any more than He did with the disciples.**

selves with each other becomes a barrier and causes us to lose focus. We can learn from the successes and failures of other followers, including the twelve, but Jesus is our leader. We must listen to him intently for instructions.

Jimy Williams, now the manager of the Boston Red Sox was the third base coach for the Atlanta Braves for many of the great years for the Braves. One day he explained what was involved in the decision for a base runner to steal a base. He said:

> The runner dictates it.
> The pitcher dictates it.
> The catcher dictates it.
> The score dictates it.
> The situation dictates it.
> But I'm the dictator.[3]

Like a base stealer listening to a coach, we take our cues from the One whom we follow. Regardless of other voices, He tells us when to head for the next base.

Next, we will look at adjustments necessary as we follow Jesus. You are doing great so far—don't get weary now. Also, get ready to consider the barrier of unrealistic expectations. Before long, you will be thinking about graduation with a degree in followology.

Notes
1. Paul Powell, *Getting the Lead Out of Leadership* (Tyler, TX.: Paul Powell, 1997), 55.
2. Adapted from an illustration in my files, gleaned from a source without attribution.
3. Powell, 65.

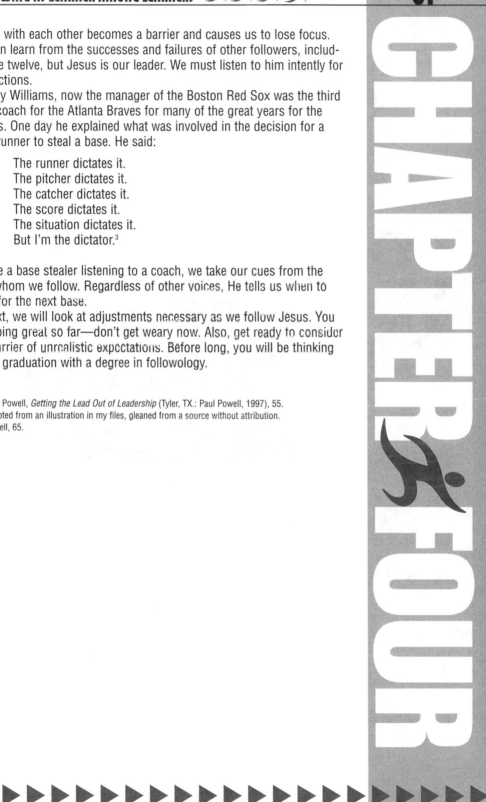

CHAPTER FOUR

CHAPTER FOUR

GREAT! YOU'RE STILL FOLLOWING!

C H A P T E R   F I V E

FOLLOWING WITH ADJUSTING EXPECTATIONS

Followology Principle: *The Choice Principle describes our responsibility to follow.*
Followology Barrier: *Spiritual Pride (Followers acknowledge that they need their leaders.)*

The long-awaited words were finally pronounced. The announcement came over the loudspeaker, "TWA Flight 924 now ready for boarding. All confirmed passengers holding a seat assignment are asked to board at this time . . ." Paris awaited. Home of the Eiffel Tower and the famous

CHAPTER FIVE

museum that sounds like "loove" but that is actually spelled "Louvre." The Champs Elysées, Arc de Triomphe, Notre Dame—all were postcard sights that Kim had dreamed about. Now she was at the gigantic (and rude) JFK airport in New York City, clutching the travel folder Dr. Wright had given her only moments before.

Dr. Wright was an expert on French culture. She was brilliant, articulate, and fluent in French, as well as three other languages. Each year, Dr. Wright selected 10 students who were juniors majoring in international studies. The group would go to Paris for a month during Christmas break. The trip, open *only* to juniors, was free. Read: no cost. Anti-dinero. All Kim had done was write an essay and fill out some forms, and the grant money Dr. Wright had secured was available.

Kim's secret ambition was to graduate in international studies and land an internship at the United States Consulate in Paris. She had taken four years of French in high school, two more years in college, and had even minored in sociology so she would have a better understanding of other cultures. She really didn't doubt that she would be chosen to go, but she was a little surprised when Dr. Wright approached her before she could even apply. Her major professor's words inflated her ego to the point of bursting. "Kim, you are the type of student I had in mind when this study grant was approved. Please consider submitting an application." Please consider? Consider it done!

Dr. Wright was also her role model. Kim could see snagging the internship, moving into a permanent position either in Paris or in New York with the United Nations, working for a few years while she completed her doctorate, and becoming a professor at a university. Her admiration for her mentor only grew when Dr. Wright asked Kim to be her office assistant, helping with typing, filing, and even some cataloging of the array of treasures the professor had collected from many trips abroad. The items were labeled and shelved according to which lecture Dr. Wright would use them for. She often taught using "show and tell."

From the time Kim received her acceptance letter, she had been making adjustments to her usual Christmas break plans. She collected clothes appropriate for Parisian weather in December. She read a couple of French novels. She went to the campus library and logged on to the Internet. She downloaded a map of Paris (cool!!!) and got the scoop on the American consulate. She planned to get over to the consulate for an interview while she was with the group in Europe. She told nobody—not even Dr. Wright—about that part of her planned itinerary.

During her search, Kim also found an article that served as a major reality check. The article read,

> On the evening of Wednesday, July 17, 1996, TWA Flight 800, carrying 212 passengers and 17 crew members, exploded and crashed into the Atlantic Ocean off the coast of Long Island shortly after taking off from New York City's John F. Kennedy International Airport en route to Paris. There were no survivors, and at this time the cause of the crash has not been determined.

Kim linked to another related site with this story:

An official with the airline told the press that the plane, a Boeing 747, had disappeared from radar and radio contact at 8:40 p.m. EDT. Asked if there had been anything unusual about Flight 800, the official responded, "Everything looked perfectly normal for the departure of an international flight."

Coast Guard officials said the plane appeared to have gone into the sea about eight to 10 miles offshore to the south of the village of Center Moriches, which is on the southeast Long Island coast about 70 miles east of Manhattan and several miles west of Westhampton. Numerous witnesses reported hearing at least one explosion before seeing a fireball fall into the sea.

Finally, she linked to a story which chilled her to the bone:

Twenty-one people (16 students and 5 adults) from Montoursville, Pennsylvania, population 5,000, also perished in the TWA Flight 800 crash in July, 1996. Blue and gold ribbon representing the Montoursville High School colors are being worn in the small town as a symbol to show support for the families and friends affected by this loss.

The youth and adults were on a study trip to Paris as a part of the Montoursville High School French Club. They hoped to visit the sites which had previously been studied in books and travel guides . . . condolences had arrived by email from all over the world.[1]

Now all of a sudden, the cost seemed higher. In fact, two students had dropped out as a result of the disaster on Flight 800. Nonetheless, Kim had made all the necessary preparations, secured her visa, saved spending money, and, oh yes, found out the address of the American consulate—2 Avenue Gabriel, Paris, France. Actually, it was the United States *Embassy*. Boy, did that have a nice ring to it. She could see herself now in a tailored business suit, reporting for work. *Oui!*

When the group landed in Paris, Dr. Wright must have assumed they got all the sleep needed on the overnight flight. When they landed, they landed running. The postcard sights became a blur, and Kim's plan to go by the Embassy during free time wasn't looking good. Dr. Wright was fascinating to listen to as she described in detail all the intricacies of Paris one could not glean unless visiting this internationally famous city. Each day, Kim revised her plans as free time looked like less and less of a possibility.

On day three, Kim saw her chance: three hours of unplanned time after lunch! Quickly, she contacted the desk at the hotel and made sure a taxi would be available. She knew she needed to talk to Dr. Wright about her plan—she couldn't just disappear. Kim caught the professor right after breakfast. Before she could say anything, however, Dr. Wright spoke up. "I have been wanting to talk to you about something. Would you mind eating lunch with me and then going by the International University to help me with some research while the others are touring on their own?" The look in Dr. Wright's eyes told Kim that "no" would disappoint her mentor.

Kim's frustration grew. As she ate with Dr. Wright that afternoon, she said little. Later, in the coffee shop at the university, her favorite professor finally got to the point. Dr. Wright dropped the bombshell: "Kim, after you graduate, would you consider coming to Paris to be my research assistant? I am writing a book during my sabbatical from our university, and my husband and I are moving here for one year. I would like to hire you for that year to do research and to interact with the academic community here in Paris. You would also work closely with the United States Ambassador's staff to secure clearances for us to travel to other parts of France to gather background. You could live with us, so your expenses would be minimal."

Suddenly the visit to the consulate didn't seem all that important.

▲Chat Room▲▲▲▲▲▲▲▲▲▲▲▲▲

How was the trip motivating Kim? Jot down two ideas.
1.
2.

Did she make any adjustments before the trip even started?
❑ Yes   ❑ No

Identify one of her expectations:
1.

What do you think her professor would have said if Kim had turned down her lunch invitation with an excuse that she "wanted to do some sightseeing"? Check the ones you feel apply.

❑ You have to go home
❑ You have to have lunch with me
❑ I'm disappointed in you

❑ Enjoy your sighseeing
❑ You need to adjust your schedule
❑ I have something to tell you

List two things Kim would have missed if she had not made some adjustments to her schedule and her expectations.
1.
2.

▲▲▲▲▲▲▲▲▲▲▲▲▲▲▲▲▲▲▲▲▲

IMITATION AND ADJUSTMENT

The Adjustment Principle describes level four in followology. Followers who are motivated to follow a leader assume the responsibility for choosing their leader and develop the discipline of focusing on their leader. Then they must nurture an attitude of submission to that leader. The leader determines the agenda and sets the schedule and the pace. The follower must adjust. In a way, the Adjustment Principle is about imitation.

Doug Berky is one of the best mimes in the country. At a youth retreat I attended, I was amazed and amused by his mimed imitation of a chimpanzee. Doug explained how he got so good at impersonating a monkey. He said he went to the zoo and observed. And he observed. And he observed. He sat there until he could predict what the monkeys would do next, based on watching them for hours. He sketched their features for a mask that he would create. By the time he finished perfecting his "monkey act," the students at the youth retreat were convinced that Doug had become a monkey! He said that in the same way, we should be imitators of Christ. To do that, we should spend time observing what He does, how He acts, and how He reacts. Then, maybe people who look at us will be convinced we have become like Him, too.[2]

SPIRITUAL GROWTH

It is difficult being a reflection. It is difficult to imitate a monkey. In both situations, the follower, or imitator, must give up control. The follower must make whatever adjustments are necessary to copy the movements of the leader. If we imitate someone long enough, we are able to anticipate the next movement, because we begin to actually think like the other person. We begin to learn their attitudes. As followers, we are not in control.

Lots of people are willing to follow Jesus if they can specify the terms. That goes for Phase Two followers just as surely as it applied to Phase One followers. These followers will gladly join the cause—if the leader will adjust to their wants or needs. Usually, the adjustment expected of the leader is not drastic. Agreements are made to be negotiated. Yet such negotiation of conditions always indicates a battle for control. Who will be in charge?

During His earthly ministry, Jesus invited lots of people to follow Him. At first, the number of disciples was large. A few of those Phase One followers, however, allowed us to see the challenge of developing an attitude of unconditional spiritual submission to Jesus' leadership in the lives of Phase Two followers. In this section of your study, you will discover the truths in the Scripture. I will give you the heading, and you define it according to details found in the verses indicated. Following your research, brief comments will follow.

Adjusting by Dealing with Unspoken Conditions

> Then a teacher of the law came to him and said, "Teacher, I will follow you wherever you go." Jesus replied, "Foxes have holes and birds of the air have nests, but the Son of Man has no place to lay his head" (Matt. 8:19-20).

Examine the Scripture again and answer the two questions:

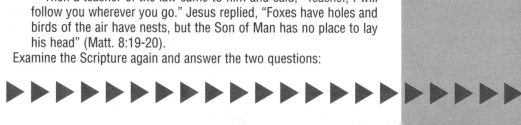

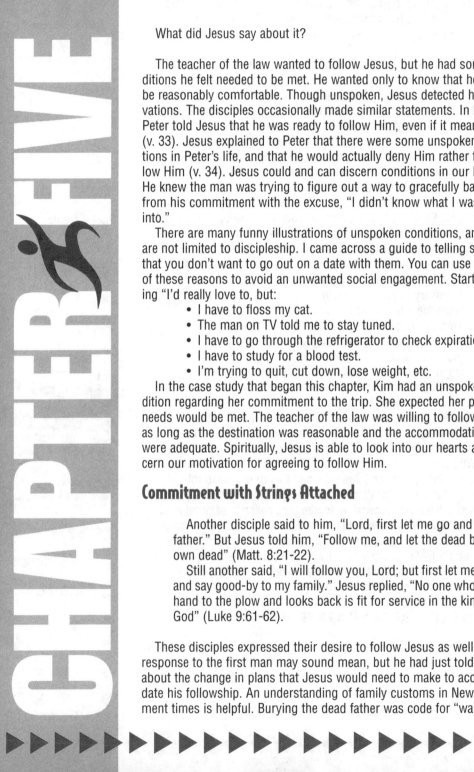

What did the man indicate about his willingness to follow?

What did Jesus say about it?

The teacher of the law wanted to follow Jesus, but he had some conditions he felt needed to be met. He wanted only to know that he would be reasonably comfortable. Though unspoken, Jesus detected his reservations. The disciples occasionally made similar statements. In Luke 22, Peter told Jesus that he was ready to follow Him, even if it meant death (v. 33). Jesus explained to Peter that there were some unspoken conditions in Peter's life, and that he would actually deny Him rather than follow Him (v. 34). Jesus could and can discern conditions in our hearts. He knew the man was trying to figure out a way to gracefully back away from his commitment with the excuse, "I didn't know what I was getting into."

There are many funny illustrations of unspoken conditions, and they are not limited to discipleship. I came across a guide to telling someone that you don't want to go out on a date with them. You can use any one of these reasons to avoid an unwanted social engagement. Start by saying "I'd really love to, but:

- I have to floss my cat.
- The man on TV told me to stay tuned.
- I have to go through the refrigerator to check expiration dates.
- I have to study for a blood test.
- I'm trying to quit, cut down, lose weight, etc.

In the case study that began this chapter, Kim had an unspoken condition regarding her commitment to the trip. She expected her personal needs would be met. The teacher of the law was willing to follow Jesus as long as the destination was reasonable and the accommodations were adequate. Spiritually, Jesus is able to look into our hearts and discern our motivation for agreeing to follow Him.

Commitment with Strings Attached

> Another disciple said to him, "Lord, first let me go and bury my father." But Jesus told him, "Follow me, and let the dead bury their own dead" (Matt. 8:21-22).
> Still another said, "I will follow you, Lord; but first let me go back and say good-by to my family." Jesus replied, "No one who puts his hand to the plow and looks back is fit for service in the kingdom of God" (Luke 9:61-62).

These disciples expressed their desire to follow Jesus as well. His response to the first man may sound mean, but he had just told Jesus about the change in plans that Jesus would need to make to accommodate his followship. An understanding of family customs in New Testament times is helpful. Burying the dead father was code for "wait for my inheritance," and saying goodbye to the family was similar. Further investigation into the family commitments that these persons professed to have reveals that they were little more than the smoky haze of good intentions. The first man's father probably was not even dead yet and the second probably envisioned a lengthy goodbye (as in years) before he was ready to follow Jesus. Family commitments are not bad things. Jesus wasn't trying to help us see that discipleship is a choice between a good life and a bad life. Many would-be disciples are good people, with lives filled with good things. *Jesus was trying to help us see that we must choose between what is good and what is best.* Think about your motivation for saying no to engagements. Perhaps you are already overcommitted. Maybe you are the kind of person who can't say no to anyone. Maybe you don't want to hurt someone's feelings. These reasons are even more intense when they involve family.

> Jesus was trying to help us see that we must choose between what is good and what is best.

Excuses Disguised as Conditions

> But they all alike began to make excuses. The first said, "I have just bought a field, and I must go and see it. Please excuse me." Another said, "I have just bought five yoke of oxen, and I'm on my way to try them out. Please excuse me." Still another said, "I just got married, so I can't come" (Luke 14:18-20).

What did the man who bought a field indicate about his willingness to follow?

These guys in Scripture are a little different from the first two mentioned in the earlier Scripture. Rational reasons have been replaced with flimsy excuses. List their excuses and try to come up with a modern-day parallel. As an example, here is the first one:

Excuse #1:   I just bought a field I need to look at.
Modern day: I need to take care of my new car.

Excuse #2:
Modern Day:

Excuse #3:
Modern day:

Wow! We've heard them all before! Society in general has become expert in excuse making and blame assigning. If we get a traffic ticket, we blame the policeman for being mean. If we hear about an accident, our first response is, Whose fault was it? A comic strip in the newspaper pokes fun at the little ghost who runs around the house and causes

havoc. The name of the ghost is "Not Me." Any time someone in the cartoon family wants to know, "Who is responsible for . . .?" the little ghost runs away, and Not Me gets the blame. Many Christians are experts in spiritual excuse making and blame assigning. No matter what they are asked to do in growth or service, they respond with a spiritual-sounding excuse. I have identified some ways that excuses distract:

1. Excuses shift focus away from what really matters—(first excuse in Luke 9). Today's equivalent would be an investment—but it would be absurd to invest in a field (or anything else) and *then* go look at it. The man didn't want to go.

2. Excuses cause you to lose perspective (second excuse)—road test *oxen*? The true issue is forgotten.

3. Excuses reveal fear—we nervously avoid commitment. All of the excuses were particularly nuts, because even if they were reasonable, what was the hurry?

4. Excuses paralyze the ability to make decisions.

To further illustrate the ridiculous nature of our excuses and conditions, enjoy a list of excuses for refusing to take blame. These came off actual claims forms submitted to an insurance company!

- Coming home, I drove into the wrong driveway and collided with a tree I don't have.
- The pedestrian had no idea which direction to go, so I ran over him.
- I backed into my neighbor's parked car. It wasn't my fault—he was supposed to be at work.
- My car was legally parked as I backed into the other vehicle.
- The guy was all over the road—I had to swerve a number of times before I hit him.
- I pulled away from the side of the road, glanced at my mother-in-law, and headed over the embankment.
- The telephone pole was approaching fast. I was attempting to swerve out of its path when it struck my front end.

The Adjustment Principle tells us Jesus wants us to know what we are getting into and adjust other things to accommodate His priorities. This is hard. Rather than memorizing Scripture (we have too much studying to do already) or sharing the story of Jesus with a classmate (they have a right to their own opinions), we supply excuses.

▲Chat Room▲▲▲▲▲▲▲▲▲▲▲▲▲

Can people be disciples while constantly giving excuses for why they cannot follow Jesus? Check your answer:

❑ Yes   ❑ No   ❑ Maybe   ❑ I don't think so

What excuses have you given for not submitting to spiritual disciplines (memorizing Scripture, witnessing, praying)? Can you jot down two?

1.

2.

What adjustments can you make to sell out to following Jesus right now? Use the space below to list your adjustments.

▲▲▲▲▲▲▲▲▲▲▲▲▲▲▲▲▲▲

As Phase Two followers, we potentially described pitfalls of Phase One followers just studied. In an emotional moment, we have declared loyalty to the cause of Christ before our intentions have been tested either physically or spiritually. It is easy to say we will follow Jesus as long as our career plans are on track, our family life is stable, and our future is relatively predictable. If our definition of discipleship involves a minimum daily requirement of commitment, we have missed it. Jesus never said it would be easy, and the privilege of discipleship certainly isn't cheap.

The Bible tells us that we must be sold out, prayed up, cost counting, faith-walking disciples. Anything less is not an imitation of Christ, but imitation discipleship. Be sure to note the difference. There will always be seemingly rational reasons to give Jesus our full devotion at a later time in our life—after college, after we marry, after we have children, after we settle into a career. We have no right to negotiate the terms under which we will be disciples. Jesus is the leader. As His followers, we must make the adjustments.

FOLLOWOLOGY BARRIER: UNREALISTIC EXPECTATIONS

If the road is going to get rough in spots, isn't it better to know up front? Then your expectations will be more realistic. Beware any diet plan stating that you can lose 18 inches off your waist in 6 hours. Take caution with any commercial which ends with the promise that "operators are standing by." Don't get your hopes up with a car wax promising that you don't have to rub very hard. If something is worthwhile, it likely involves time, effort, or both. The notable exception is the grace Jesus extends for our salvation. He gives it freely. It is possible that in your youth-group days, you were told that becoming a Christian was easy. And it is. But the demands of continuing discipleship and obedience may or may not have been clearly communicated. Unrealistic expectations create major obstacles with discipleship.

▶▶▶▶▶▶▶▶▶▶▶▶▶▶▶▶▶▶▶▶

Jesus told people the truth about discipleship, describing the challenges as well as the benefits. He welcomed all to follow, but He never said it would be easy. He promised Peter that Satan would "sift him like wheat" (Luke 22:31). He appeared to be trying to talk the persons described in your Scripture study above *out* of following Him. Not so. He simply wanted them to know what they were in for. Look up the illustration He gave to nail this point.

"Suppose one of you wants to build a tower. Will he not first sit down and estimate the cost to see if he has enough money to complete it? For if he lays the foundation and is not able to finish it, everyone who sees it will ridicule him, saying, 'This fellow began to build and was not able to finish'" (Luke 14:28-30).

Jesus knew that God had placed in each of us a need to be committed to something. Look around you in college. It seems like everyone is protesting something or speaking up for something else. Steve Masters is the director of Baptist student ministry at Louisiana State University and a friend of mine. In a conversation with Steve, I asked him about "Free Speech Alley" at LSU. He told me there was an area of campus so designated. Whenever anyone desired to give a speech, they climb up on an outdoor platform, and soon they would draw a crowd. I expressed my amazement to Steve that college students would be that bold, and that others would actually stop and listen.

▲Chat Room▲▲▲▲▲▲▲▲▲▲▲▲

If you gave a speech for Jesus in "Free Speech Alley," what would be your topic?

What would be the main points of your talk?

Jesus also knew that eventually people would figure out that discipleship was a cause worth the cost. Look up Matthew 13:44-46. In both stories, people found something of great value and sacrificed greatly to obtain it. The spiritual application is that they understood the great value of a relationship with God. Unfortunately, the consumer mentality of our modern culture obscures this truth. We are told we can buy things to make life easier or better, but when we buy those items, we should "never pay retail." Ask for a discount. The danger is for us to dabble in consumer Christianity. Worse yet, some people act out their followship like my children play with Christmas toys in February. My daughter's "Giga Pet" is no longer receiving the care it did the last week in December! Some disciples, like the man who built the tower, start strong, but fizzle out. Jesus wants us to finish strong, after counting the cost. He said (to them all): "If anyone would come after me, he must deny himself and take up his cross daily and follow me" (Luke 9:23). Someone else said, "If the cause is great enough, the cost is irrelevant." Jesus wants to clarify our expectations so we can make a decision to follow Him. We cannot settle for anything less or expect anything easier. We cannot discount that for which Jesus died. For such a prize, no price is too great.

Adjustments in and out of Center Field

The Los Angeles Dodgers jersey with number 22 on it was too clean. Its usual wearer routinely stained that jersey with diving head-first slides to catch fly balls as he roamed his turf in center field at Dodger stadium. Brett Butler left his jersey there to get an insignificant tonsillectomy. On May 3, 1996, however, Butler heard his doctor say the *C* word. On May 21, the doctors went back in to remove cancerous lymph nodes from his throat.[3]

I sat beside Brett Butler at a minor league baseball game in August of 1996. I am the chaplain for the AAA (minor league) team in New Orleans, and Butler was there to rehabilitate and recondition, preparing to return to his spot in the Dodger lineup. He spoke at chapel and expressed a faith in God that was inspirational to the team. He told how he trusted God, and worked incredibly hard to make it back to the big game in spite of the doctors' prognosis that it would be nearly impossible.

On September 6, 1996, Brett Butler returned to the familiar center field to a thundering ovation. He had a great game, contributing a hit, the game-winning run, and a stolen base to a Dodgers victory. On September 10 of the same week, Butler was hit by a pitch that broke his left hand. His season was over. His expectations were unrealistic by many standards and through the disappointment, he learned something. *He learned that he needed to surrender even more control of his life to God.* I will tell you the rest of Brett Butler's story when we talk about the next barrier—understanding the purpose of testing. For now, observe how Butler adjusted his expectations to follow Jesus. He could have protested to God, saying, "But I can be such a witness in major league baseball!" He didn't and doesn't understand all the reasons behind his journey, but he has chosen to adjust his life to more closely follow the Leader.

> He learned that he needed to surrender even more control of his life to God.

Now let's get specific. What practical adjustments can college students make to follow Jesus? More specifically, what adjustments will you make? Close out your study of the Adjustment Principle and the Unrealistic Expectation Barrier with a journal entry.

▲Chat Room▲ ▲ ▲ ▲ ▲ ▲ ▲ ▲ ▲ ▲ ▲ ▲

If all you have read is true, name some ways you will have to make adjustments at school with:

How I use my time
1.
2.

How I spend my money
1.
2.

My dating life
1.
2.

My social activities
1.
2.

My college major
1.
2.

My studies
1.
2.

▲▲▲▲▲▲▲▲▲▲▲▲▲▲▲▲▲▲▲▲

That was a tough chapter. Next, we will examine the joy of discipleship as viewed through the lens of a relationship with your Leader. Once you have paid the price of paying attention to the Leader, of maintaining your spiritual focus, and of developing an attitude of submission, the rewards are immense. The barriers may even become a little less intimidating.

Notes

1. The facts of the tragic incident are true. The account here is gleaned from numerous newspapers, magazines, and Internet sites.
2. Doug Berky spoke at the Georgia Baptist Discipleship Department Winter Retreat in Pigeon Forge, Tennessee, January 1998.
3. My conversation with Brett Butler took place in New Orleans. Details of his incredible story were found in "Extra Innings," by Rob Bentz, *Stand Firm* magazine, April 1997, 5-6.

C H A P T E R   S I X

FOLLOWING COMES NATURALLY

Followology Principle: *The Relationship Principle describes the nature of following.*
Followology Barrier: *Misunderstood Purpose (Testing while following enhances learning.)*

Bob was the intern to the student minister at the local church. Okay, so he was *one* of the interns. The church used the internship program to assist with ministry to college students. The church was in the same town as a major state university, and during the school year, the college department was quite large. The last line on the job description should have read, "and other duties that nobody else wants to do." The hours were horrendous. The pay was lousy. All four interns shared an office. Rather, they shared a cubicle—okay a desk. And they loved every minute of it.

CHAPTER SIX

There were four of them. Bob was a junior majoring in education administration. Paula was a senior majoring in childhood education. Jeanine, a junior, was the social work major, and Jerry was a sophomore whose major of the week was psychology (last week it was polymer science). The common thread among them was their relationship with Chuck. Chuck was the student minister at the church. The "fantastic four" had met him while he was youth minister in their home church, located in a small town in the southern part of the state. That was back when they were in high school. Chuck had been at this church for four years, and now that they were in college, it seemed natural that they would all be together again.

Chuck had discipled students regularly as part of youth ministry. When the opportunity came for him to move into a ministry in a university town with duties including college students, he was excited. He had felt most effective when working with students who were relatively focused. The university setting allowed him to minister to students about to step into any number of vocations. Chuck's goal was to help infiltrate businesses, schools, government—sending graduates of the university into the real world. He was always proud when a student "surrendered to ministry," but he also envisioned the secular workplace salted with graduates who were Christian—students who had been discipled and were not afraid to take their witness into the marketplace. His four interns had been part of that discipleship process since high school. They all showed real promise, but Chuck was beginning to feel like they needed to be challenged a bit more.

At first, Bob and the other three interns did little more than follow Chuck around. He met with them once a week for "staff discipleship." They had gone through various books on discipleship. They also memorized Scripture, and their prayer times were becoming more and more meaningful. They went with him as he led dorm Bible studies, assisted him with planning the "Back to School Bash," "Fall Phenomenon," and "Mudbowl for Missions." It was great fun for them to be the logistics team, generally working behind the scenes. Occasionally, one of them would speak, giving a testimony or a short devotional, but Chuck would always be there for them.

This time, though, Chuck wasn't around. He had taken the college students from the church to a challenge conference, leaving the fab four to conduct a spring retreat for the junior high youth at the church. They had gained confidence over the nine months with Chuck, so they felt like they could pull it off. Chuck had supervised as they planned carefully. Bob took care of the schedule. Paula was in charge of recreation. Jerry would lead music. Jeanine would assemble the curriculum for small groups. They would share the speaking responsibilities. They all had already prepared their Bible study talk and practiced it in front of the others. They were on their game!

From the beginning, things started to go wrong. Some parents wanted alternate transportation arrangements so their kids could attend the band concert Friday night. Others informed the interns they would need

to pick up their teenager early to attend a family obligation. The "leadership by committee" was tested when another parent demanded to know, "Who's in charge here?" The order from the food distributor was late, some permission forms appeared to have forged notary signatures, and there was a possible conflict with one of the church vans. If it could go wrong, it did.

The four interns met for prayer and decision-making. Chuck had gradually given them greater and greater responsibility. He had moved to the background as they had tried their wings in ministry. As they prayed, they realized they had been given opportunities over the past year that had been like sectional tests, checking progress on abilities in leadership and ministry. Though they were comforted by the realization that they probably could get through this thing, they sure wished Chuck were there.

▲ Chat Room ▲▲▲▲▲▲▲▲▲▲▲▲

Was Chuck systematic about his discipleship with the interns? (One line answer to either answer.)

Yes! How?

No! Why?

Jot down one lesson you think Jeanine and the others learned through their experience with the food collection project.

1.

Was Chuck being fair when he left the interns in charge of the retreat? Why or why not? Think about your answer. Briefly, write it down below.

Which of Christ's disciples do you feel the interns were like?

Bob was like _____

Paula was like _____

Jeanine was like _____

Jerry was like _____

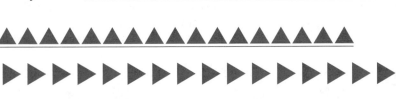

FOLLOWING PRODUCES RELATIONSHIPS

The Relationship Principle, simply stated, means that following produces relationships. The followism is stated: *Following builds relationships.* The interns in the story could not have experienced

CHRISTLIKE
RELATIONSHIPS

all they did together without developing a sense of community with each other. That community, however, was centered around their relationship with Chuck. He had recognized a gift of leadership in each of them, and he chose them to be his interns when the opportunity presented itself.

As followologists, you can readily make the spiritual application. So far, we have discussed four principles of followology. If we want to be better followers of Jesus, we can apply:

- **The Need Principle.**—We want to follow if we feel like we are missing something that can be obtained by following. We recognize we don't know the way.
- **The Choice Principle.**—We are responsible for following the right leader. We will experience negative consequences if we choose the wrong leader. We choose to follow Jesus.
- **The Focus Principle.**—Even if we want to follow the right leader, we have to pay attention to keep the leader in sight. We make Jesus the central focus in our lives.
- **The Adjustment Principle.**—To continue following, we have to adjust our lives to make sure we stay behind the leader. We develop a submissive attitude by adjusting our lives to whatever Jesus tells us to do.

The four principles up to this point have to do with responsiveness of the follower. These last three principles deal with the results of continued, disciplined following. Imagine yourself in a car, driving through an unfamiliar city. You are in a line of cars and you are following your guide in the car ahead of you. You know you need to follow her because she knows the way, and you do not. You have chosen to follow her and no other, because you do not know where all those other cars will end up. You are watching closely to make sure they don't exit without you.

Somewhere in here, you become more and more comfortable with the speed at which they are driving, their driving habits, and so forth. You feel like you can anticipate their moves. (Remember the followology principle in Chapter 1? The better you know the leader, the easier it becomes to follow.) Now you are enjoying the drive. You have started to see progress. You have changed into a more confident follower, and feel you will reach the destination any moment now.

Both leader and follower are more familiar with one another. As followers of Jesus, we understand that the disciplines of choosing (daily!) and paying attention give way to the intimate relationship we have with Him. Slowly, but surely, we are changed. In the book on which this one was based, John Kramp makes a profound statement:

This relationship [with Jesus] elevates Christianity beyond all other religions, philosophies, and worldviews. The God who created the world says we get to know Him, talk with Him, walk with Him. In a way, God lets us "hang around" with Him. How? By following. That's how Jesus built the relationships with His first followers. By studying what He did then, we can learn how Jesus wants us to follow Him today.[1]

Relationships with Gen X Followers

The relationship that one can have with Jesus is the key to the radical difference with Jesus. It is also what will appeal to any Generation X college students who have "seen it all." Here are some reasons a relationship with Jesus is appealing to your generation:[2]

- A person is at the center of the faith.
- The ethical teachings are fair and make sense.
- Following Jesus is the only religion in the world where God takes the initiative.
- Authentic—Christianity is the only religion in the world where the deity died for the people.
- Obedience is a response, not a condition. We follow because we are Christians, not so we can become Christians.
- Jesus promises and delivers resources to help us follow throughout our earthly lives.

▲Chat Room▲▲▲▲▲▲▲▲▲▲▲▲▲

Using ideas from the list above, write a script explaining followology in terms of relationship. Pretend that someone has asked you to explain the difference between Jesus and any other great spiritual teacher. Put your script in your own words.

▲▲▲▲▲▲▲▲▲▲▲▲▲▲▲▲▲▲▲▲

What a great time to be a follower of Jesus! The truth the disciples discovered—that following Jesus is not a religion but a relationship—is the most appealing aspect of Christianity as we look into the third millennium. In addition to the benefit of being in a relationship with Jesus, following Jesus provides purpose. The teachings of Jesus make sense. Our world is full of contradictions and complications. The simple,

straightforward teachings of Jesus are refreshingly simple. Here is a sample from the Sermon on the Mount:

"Simply let your 'Yes' be 'Yes,' and your 'No,' 'No'; anything beyond this comes from the evil one" (Matt. 5:37).

"Do not store up for yourselves treasures on earth, where moth and rust destroy, and where thieves break in and steal. But store up for yourselves treasures in heaven, where moth and rust do not destroy, and where thieves do not break in and steal" (Matt. 6:19-20).

"Therefore I tell you, do not worry about your life, what you will eat or drink; or about your body, what you will wear. Is not life more important than food, and the body more important than clothes?" (Matt. 6:25).

"Do not judge, or you too will be judged" (Matt. 7:1).

Relationship, Not Religion

Good stuff—but they aren't rules. Look more closely at the teachings in the verses above. They are the kinds of things said to a good friend who needs some direction in life. They are **relationship** principles, not **religion** principles.

A moment ago, I also mentioned that following Jesus gives direction and purpose. Jesus had a job for the Phase One followers. Look for the three objectives that were a part of the mission statement Jesus left for the twelve:

He appointed twelve—designating them apostles—that they might be with him and that he might send them out to preach and to have authority to drive out demons (Mark 3:14-15; this is also found in Matt. 10:8).

▲Chat Room▲▲▲▲▲▲▲▲▲▲▲▲▲▲

What does the CrossSeekers icon "Christlike Relationships" mean to you in the context of this study? Jot down one or two thoughts.

1.

2.

Pick one. If you were a disciple back then, and Jesus had just told you these things, you would

(a) say, "Cool, but when do we see the demons?"

(b) ask, "If we get tired, are there twelve more you are going to pick?"

(c) declare, "Well, let's get started. There are a lot of people on this planet to preach to."

(d) pray, "Only in the strength of a relationship with You could I ever do a job that big."

Now find what the disciples did. Look in Matthew 11:1.

▲▲▲▲▲▲▲▲▲▲▲▲▲▲▲▲▲▲▲▲

Okay, so that last one wasn't fair. All the Bible says is that He (Jesus) departed from there to teach and to preach. You have to read a bit further to see that the disciples were with Him (see Matt. 12:1). How is it that after Jesus left, the disciples were still with Him? Remember from a few chapters ago? If Jesus left and showed up at another place, and the disciples were with Him before He got to the new place and after He got to the new place, *then they must have followed Him*. They answered, *d* above.

Jesus wanted them to preach. He gave them authority to do the job. He counted on the strength of the relationship that He had with them to motivate, equip, and provide courage to get the job done. He placed all His heavenly eggs in the earthly basket of relationship. Consider a skit that I wrote (and others have probably written other versions!) based on a story passed around for years.

The Great Commission Revisited

Angel: Welcome back to heaven, Jesus. We sure have missed you these 33 years.

Jesus: It is good to be back.

Angel: Did you get everything straightened out down there?

Jesus: I think so.

Angel: Did you enlist a great army to eliminate sin and rise up and give glory to God?

Jesus: My purpose was not to make war, but to bring peace.

Angel: (embarrassed) Oh, I forgot. So, did you strategically place thousands of people around the world who could make laws and enforce them to ensure that peace would last forever?

Jesus: No. Remember that Moses came to bring the law. I went to fulfill it.

Angel: (more embarrassed) Oh. Yes, that's right. So, how did you carry out the Father's plan to share His message with the world?

Jesus: I asked twelve ordinary men to follow me for three years, to get to know me, to learn all that the Father

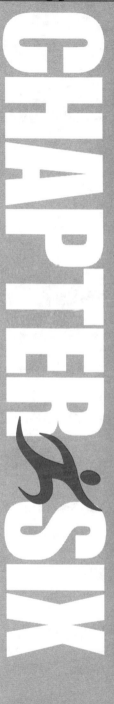

CHAPTER SIX

▶▶▶▶▶▶▶▶▶▶▶▶▶▶▶▶▶▶▶▶▶

wished them to know, then to tell others the story by preaching it.

Angel: And God transformed them into twelve great world leaders?

Jesus: No, actually, one of them betrayed me, and the other eleven got off to a slow start. But they are showing some promise now.

Angel: But what if they fail? What is the backup plan for making God's love known?

Jesus: (firmly) I HAVE NO OTHER PLAN.

Narrator: (Read Matthew 28:18-20.)

Ingredients for Relationships

Jesus' only plan was to reach the world through relationships. He and the disciples related to each other. The relationship developed over the course of the three years they were together. Like relationships you develop, certain ingredients contributed to the strength of that relationship.

I imagine you can list a bunch: things like time, communication, and shared experiences. Jesus modeled all of the above. A typical pattern is this: Jesus and the twelve are walking along, sharing life experiences when Jesus stops to minister or to teach. Usually, the disciples watch or listen. Later, He takes great care to make sure His disciples understand both the earthly meaning and the heavenly significance of what they have just witnessed. With a highlighter, mark each of those "ingredients" as well as the pattern in this passage:

> That same day Jesus went out of the house and sat by the lake. Such large crowds gathered around him that he got into a boat and sat in it, while all the people stood on the shore. Then he told them many things in parables, saying: "A farmer went out to sow his seed. As he was scattering the seed, some fell along the path, and the birds came and ate it up. Some fell on rocky places, where it did not have much soil. It sprang up quickly, because the soil was shallow. But when the sun came up, the plants were scorched, and they withered because they had no root. Other seed fell among thorns, which grew up and choked the plants. Still other seed fell on good soil, where it produced a crop—a hundred, sixty or thirty times what was sown. He who has ears, let him hear." The disciples came to him and asked, "Why do you speak to the people in parables?" He replied, "The knowledge of the secrets of the kingdom of heaven has been given to you, but not to them" (Matt. 13:1-11).

See another key in verse 16. After telling the disciples that they were the recipients of special understanding, Jesus explained the parable to them, just to be sure. As a result of spending large amounts of time

with Jesus, the twelve began to know how He thought, how He viewed life, and how He wanted them to think and act.

Relationships Translate to Influence

Such relationship translates to influence. When I was first asked to lead chapel services for the New Orleans Zephyrs baseball team (remember, I told you they are the Houston Triple A club), approaching the locker room intimidated me. I was afraid I would be thrown out. When the manager saw me coming, he told the guy who guards the door, "He's okay. He's with the team." What incredible words. I was given influence and access upon the words of the team leader.

SPIRITUAL GROWTH

The disciples were also given influence and access. They would see how important they were to Jesus. Even when the crowds were demanding time with Jesus, He set aside private time for the disciples to ask questions. Jesus knew the strength of the relationship with His disciples was the only guarantee His influence with them would continue after He left them. I can force my son to obey me while I am in the room with him. (I am bigger than he is for now!) However, forced obedience is not influence. If my son does what he knows I would like him to do *when I am not around*, then my relationship has had influence. Jesus understood the dynamics of investing in relationships.

The relationship between Jesus and the disciples contained some other ingredients as well. They laughed together (I bet they laughed at Peter's panic when he tried to walk on water); they cried together (They saw Jesus weep over the death of His friend Lazarus); they were embarrassed together (Tell me again why we couldn't drive out those demons). These were some tender times.

▲Chat Room▲▲▲▲▲▲▲▲▲▲▲▲▲

Think about your closest relationship. Using the following emotions as a reminder, jot down a word that reminds you of an experience you have shared with your friend involving that emotion. Take your time.

Split-your-side laughter:

Sorrow too deep for words:

News so fantastic you woke them in the middle of the night:

▲▲▲▲▲▲▲▲▲▲▲▲▲▲▲▲▲▲▲▲▲

▶▶▶▶▶▶▶▶▶▶▶▶▶▶▶▶▶▶▶▶▶▶▶

Back to the Physical Metaphor

Remember the example of getting more and more comfortable following someone as you got used to their mannerisms, habits, and quirks as they drove a car in front of you? Well, modify that. Jesus isn't in the car ahead of you. He desires to be in the car *with* you, giving directions so you can follow Him. Keep following Jesus by relating to Him as a "friend that is closer than a brother," and He will give you all the directions you need.

THE BARRIER OF MISUNDERSTANDING THE PURPOSE OF TESTING

Did you ever take one of those tests to discover if you could follow directions? At the top of the page, you were instructed to write your name on the paper. The very first instruction was something like, *"READ THE TEST PAPER COMPLETELY BEFORE ANSWERING ANY QUESTIONS."* Then the page had directions telling the unsuspecting test taker to do things like singing the national anthem while holding their nose, standing on one foot while chanting a favorite cheer, holding hands with three others while playing "ring around the rosie," and holding their tongues while saying the alphabet. The last item on the paper instructs the now-exhausted group to "disregard all items except for the very first one. In other words, after putting your name on the paper and reading all of the directions, you were finished. There were always a few who followed the instructions. The others had the great fun of watching them do all those embarrassing stunts. The purpose of the test was not to embarrass anyone, but to demonstrate the value of following instructions.

As a professor at a graduate institution, I have the unpleasant task of giving exams. While in my position, I feel like it is "more blessed to give than to receive." I am constantly trying to write tests that are helpful. I truly want to find out what my students know, not what they don't know. I do my best to think of creative ways to test. Jesus, the Master Teacher, also used a variety of tests to help His students learn. The followism is this: *Testing while following enhances learning.*

Jesus' Discipleship Exams

POP TESTS
Some testing is unplanned. Teachers know when they are giving pop tests, but some tests are totally unplanned. Also called "trials," they seem entirely too difficult and usually unfair at the time. These are the tests God allows as we follow Jesus to help us grow stronger. In the next chapter, we will examine the barrier of failure, but not all testing results in failure. Jesus' half brother James would later interpret such testing:

Consider it pure joy, my brothers, whenever you face trials of

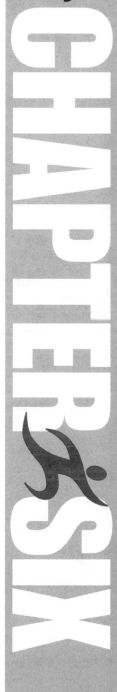

many kinds, because you know that the testing of your faith develops perseverance. Perseverance must finish its work so that you may be mature and complete, not lacking anything (Jas. 1:2-4).

When we pass such tests, we develop patience and our faith increases. It is like working out. We push muscles past the point we think we can stand, so that those muscles eventually get stronger. On Thanksgiving Day in 1996, I ran my first marathon—26 miles, 385 yards on the Olympic course in Atlanta, Georgia. Let me quickly say that I saw the Olympic course at a much slower pace than did the Olympians, but I did finish. During my training, I never ran more than 20 miles. During the race, at about mile 24, my body was screaming, "WE'VE NEVER RUN THIS FAR BEFORE!!!" When I finished, I knew my limits had been stretched, but I also knew I could finish a marathon. When the test is behind us, we are more mature in whatever area the test was in.

I told you part of the story of Los Angeles Dodgers center fielder, Brett Butler. His body became weak from the radiation treatments. When I saw him, he could never be far from a bottle of water because the radiation treatments had damaged the saliva glands in his throat which kept it moist. He didn't know if he would play baseball again. In the magazine, *Stand Firm*, Butler was quoted as saying,

> The family of God grows in love and brings everybody together in the trials and tribulations that we have. We don't get close to God when things are going good, we get close to God when things are going bad. I wish that I didn't have the cancer. But in having the cancer, I'm glad that I got it so I could grow closer to God. That's where my joy lies—in a deeper relationship with Jesus.[3]

TRUE/FALSE TESTS

In addition to the unplanned tests that come with bad weather, uncooperative people, false accusations, or internal questions each day, we also take a true/false exam. We have to answer the question, You will follow Jesus today! True or False. A daily discipleship quiz. The four fishermen from Bethsaida were faced with such a test. One day, lakeside, He performed a miracle and then tested them to see if they would follow His leadership that day.

> When he had finished speaking, he said to Simon, "Put out into deep water, and let down the nets for a catch." Simon answered, "Master, we've worked hard all night and haven't caught anything. But because you say so, I will let down the nets." When they had done so, they caught such a large number of fish that their nets began to break. So they signaled their partners in the other boat to come and help them, and they came and filled both boats so full that they began to sink. When Simon Peter saw this, he fell at Jesus' knees and said, "Go away from me, Lord; I am a sinful man!" For he and all his companions were astonished at the catch of fish they had taken, and so were James and John, the sons of Zebedee, Simon's partners. Then Jesus said to Simon, "Don't be afraid; from

WITNESS

now on you will catch men. So they pulled their boats up on shore, left everything and followed him (Luke 5:4-11).

MULTIPLE CHOICE

Sometimes the disciples were tested as they watched Jesus deal with others. In Luke 10, a teacher of the law approached Jesus to find out how little he could do to still make it into heaven. Jesus told him a para-

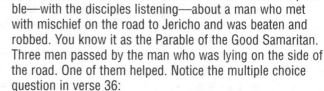

CHRISTLIKE RELATIONSHIPS

ble—with the disciples listening—about a man who met with mischief on the road to Jericho and was beaten and robbed. You know it as the Parable of the Good Samaritan. Three men passed by the man who was lying on the side of the road. One of them helped. Notice the multiple choice question in verse 36:

"Which of these three do you think was a neighbor to the man who fell into the hands of robbers?" The expert in the law replied, "The one who had mercy on him." Jesus told him, "Go and do likewise."

The lawyer guessed correctly, and the disciples breathed a sigh of relief. Then they got to hear Jesus bring home the point of the test. It wasn't enough to know the right thing to do. A gracious and generous and impartial attitude must translate knowledge into action, or the tester fails the test.

LAB QUIZ

In Luke 9:1-6, Jesus sent the disciples out on a field trip. Like the interns in the story at the beginning of the chapter, there came a time when all of the things that the disciples had learned out of their relationship with Jesus would be tested. So Jesus sent them out. He gave them authority and responsibility (both are needed if the leader expects the followers to eventually become leaders themselves). Look up Luke 9:1-6 and tackle a few questions:

SHORT ANSWER

On several occasions, Jesus tested with two short-answer questions. He was assessing how much the twelve had picked up through the relationship with Him:

Once when Jesus was praying in private and his disciples were with him, he asked them, "Who do the crowds say I am?" They replied, "Some say John the Baptist; others say Elijah; and still others, that one of the prophets of long ago has come back to life." "But what about you?" he asked. "Who do you say I am?" Peter answered, "The Christ of God" (Luke 9:18-20).

THE FINAL EXAM

Because Jesus came back from the dead, conquering death, this test was really more like the midterm exam. On the way to Jerusalem for what was to be the crucifixion, Jesus shared openly about the seriousness of the situation. They had taken lesser tests along the way. When the soldiers showed up in the garden of Gethsemane, it was time for the exit exam to see if they would be promoted. When the prospect of suffering faced them, all eleven who were with Jesus in the garden went blank. They couldn't even remember to put their names on their papers before they turned them in and ran out of class.

A Testing Program for Phase Two Disciples

I am trying to learn to test my students like God tests me. He is gentle, knowing exactly what I am capable of learning at this point in my relationship with Him. As I follow Jesus, He knows when I need to be stretched, and so He gives me tests. But those tests are always for my benefit. Consider some other subject areas in which we are tested:

- *The Stretch Test.* Are you willing to try new things for God?
- *The Servanthood Test.* Are you willing to help other followers?
- *The Contentment Test.* Are you a happy follower or a whiner?
- *The Solitude Test.* Will you follow alone if necessary?
- *The Sifting Test.* Will you follow when it is difficult?
- *The Totality Test.* Will you follow if it costs you everything?

▲Chat Room▲▲▲▲▲▲▲▲▲▲▲▲

What are some of the most significant spiritual tests you have experienced lately? Jot down in a few words two or three of them.

1.

2.

3.

What one word would describe the progress you are making? What is it?

Are you learning that you need some remedial work?
Yes ❑ No ❑ Maybe

How do you feel about spiritual tests? (Circle all that apply.)

Okay	Don't care for them	They help me
I'm not good on tests	I did great	I hate essays
They help me grow	I despise them	

▲▲▲▲▲▲▲▲▲▲▲▲▲▲▲▲▲▲▲

When we are following, we build relationships. We enjoy relationships with other followers as well as the Leader Himself. We begin to know His ways. We anticipate His direction for us. When we are tested, we are able to welcome them as opportunities to evaluate our progress and make appropriate adjustments to follow more closely. As college students, you are moving away from your support system for everyday advice. Spiritually, you are becoming adults as well. In the next chapter, we will examine the Change Principle and the Failure Barrier. Stay tuned!

Notes

1. John Kramp, *Getting Ahead by Staying Behind* (Nashville: Broadman & Holman, 1997), 50-51.
2. From a presentation on Generation X compiled from various sources by the author. Thanks to Perry Sanders, pastor of First Baptist Church of Lafayette, Louisiana, for the seed of an idea. Dr. Sanders referred to these characteristics of faith in a chapel message, delivered at the New Orleans Baptist Theological Seminary, September 10, 1996.
3. Rob Bentz, "Extra Innings," *Stand Firm*, April 1997, 6.

CHAPTER SIX

NATURALLY, YOU'RE FOLLOWING!

C H A P T E R   S E V E N

FOLLOWING ON PURPOSE

Followology Principle: *The Change Principle explains the purpose of following.*
Followology Barrier: *Failure (Those who fail can follow again.)*

He had always wanted to be a teacher. As a little boy, Brandon would play "school," teaching different subjects on different days. Sometimes his class consisted of other children in the neighborhood. For other class sessions, his mother patiently played the role of the children in his class, and on one occasion, Brandon lectured the family dog on "numbers times themselves." He would give tests, have spelling bees, even declare recess or lunch.

For his future vocation, Brandon had two role models. His mother went back to teaching when Brandon went to first grade. He loved to hear stories of how his mom helped the children—how one child was really improving, or how this student overcame a problem. His other

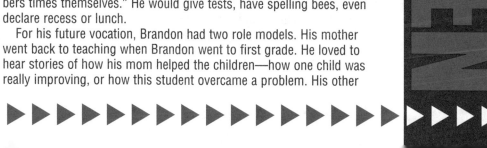

role model was his sixth grade teacher, Mrs. Clark. Before his mom decided to stay home to help Brandon and his sister with their preschool years, his mother's student teaching had been with Mrs. Clark, so she knew Brandon before he was in her class. Of course, that brought both good news and bad news. Good news because she knew to challenge him. He enjoyed extra time on the classroom computer as he waited on his mom to finish bus duty and then pick him up (when his mom returned to the classroom, she went to the high school) at the end of each school day. Bad news because Brandon couldn't get away with anything. Even when he sold the chips and snack cakes from his lunch to another boy, Brandon's mom found out. In sixth grade, Brandon knew he would one day teach like Mrs. Clark.

Brandon didn't know at the time to observe that Mrs. Clark's class was person-centered rather than content-centered. Nor did he know that, as a child, his concrete thinking patterns were giving way to abstract thought—but she knew. He couldn't have known that Mrs. Clark intentionally varied her teaching style almost daily. She used lesson plans that involved smell and taste and touch, rather than teaching exclusively in the domains of sight and hearing. It was beyond his time to be aware that she lived out what the textbooks suggested—and then some.

As the children's games gave way to the teenage years, Brandon's desire to follow his mother and Mrs. Clark into a career in the classroom remained strong. He would occasionally "get to teach." He volunteered to do the Bible story for children's church. Brandon was always on the list to help with Vacation Bible School. As a junior in high school, he was required by his school to volunteer in the community. He chose to be a tutor for inner city elementary school children. Brandon was also well-received as the teacher of the Adult 6 men's class on youth Sunday at his church.

Now Brandon was a college senior in secondary education. He hadn't really noticed that he was becoming more competent with each teaching opportunity that came along. It was a subtle change—he still thought of a teacher as something he was going to be rather than something he *was*. In the back of his mind, he knew he would be in the classroom next year, but he figured student teaching in the spring would make it more real. Ah, yes, there was student teaching. He had been told of several possibilities, and fortunately, he would be home for a week during winter break, to talk the options over with his mom.

When the phone rang on Monday of break week, and the voice on the other end belonged to the principal of his old high school, Brandon's first thought was that he was in trouble. Wait a minute! He couldn't be in trouble. He was a senior *in college*. He hadn't been in school there for four years. He focused on the principal's words. Apparently a winter flu bug had bitten one of the teachers, and she would be out for the entire week. His mother had told the principal of his availability and his interest in employment. Would Brandon be interested in substituting for the week in an English lit class? Brandon was at the high school almost before the line went dead in the principal's hand.

The week of teaching at his old school was incredible. It was a little weird, because he remembered the stuff he and his friends used to pull, and it was strange, now, being the one correcting the students. He hesitated every time he walked into the teacher's lounge, like entering forbidden territory. To his surprise and delight, the other teachers treated him like a colleague, and he felt pretty good about the week. His mom was not very vocal about it, but she was proud that her son was becoming a fine teacher. Brandon thought he saw the "light come on" in the eyes of some students, while others "tested" the substitute teacher. The principal even stopped by to watch for a few minutes. Brandon was flattered when the principal suggested that he come by the office to discuss a possible contract for the following school year. Brandon had been sent to the office before but never to discuss a job opportunity!

It wasn't until Brandon had been back at college for a few weeks that the crisis crashed in, filling his mind with doubt. While sitting in a senior English class taking an exam, his mind went completely blank.

Brandon couldn't explain why he glanced at the exam of the student next to him. He didn't cheat on tests. He knew it was fairly common, and he had even had a mental discussion with himself as to what he would do if he caught a student in his class peeking at a neighbor's paper. After he saw the list of 19th century poets, his memory was jogged, and he remembered enough to pull a B for the test. But in his heart, he knew he had cheated. He was a failure. The very thing a teacher could *not* do, he had done. He could only imagine the disappointment in his mom, Mrs. Clark—even God.

Brandon knew he needed to tell his English prof what he had done. He had not been caught. If he said nothing, he would graduate as scheduled. Even if he took an "F" in the class, he would still graduate, but according to the bulletin, there was a chance he would be suspended for cheating, thus delaying graduation by a semester. There was a slim chance that Brandon faced expulsion, but since it was the first time, he hoped and prayed for leniency. Still, he knew that if he remained silent, his integrity would have a hole in it.

The professor's response shocked Brandon. Dr. Anderson told him, "Now you are ready to be a teacher." The unexpected words gave Brandon false hope that his honesty would be rewarded with a warning, and that no further action would be taken. Then he would still have his "A" for the class, but his conscience would be clear. Not so—what Dr. Anderson meant was that he would now have compassion for the stress that his students would sometimes face, and that some would break under pressure. In this case, since he was honest, Brandon would be allowed to do a research paper to make up for the zero he would receive on the test. Fifteen pages (with footnotes) on "The Civil War Authors." Even as he trudged to the library, Brandon felt he had done the right thing.

▲Chat Room▲▲▲▲▲▲▲▲▲▲▲▲▲▲▲

Do you feel Brandon should be disqualified from being a teacher because he cheated? Why or why not?

If not, what would be "serious" enough for him to be disqualified?

▲▲▲▲▲▲▲▲▲▲▲▲▲▲▲▲▲▲▲▲▲

We Will Be Changed

We often describe someone who is spiritually lost as being saved when they accept Christ as Savior. In his book, *Out of Their Faces and into Their Shoes*, John Kramp replaces the word *saved* with the word *found* to describe the process of someone beginning a relationship with Jesus. When people are physically lost and are later found, their lives are changed by the experience. One of the most exciting things about being a minister is that I get to see this change all the time. I remember Heather (not her real name) who had a horrible reputation of sexual relationships with several different partners. She came to our youth group and accepted Christ. Fortunately, she became part of a youth group that allowed people to change, leaving the past behind. Heather got the same new start as an adulterous woman who had a life-changing (and life-saving!) encounter with Jesus:

> Jesus straightened up and asked her, "Woman, where are they? Has no one condemned you?" "No one, sir," she said. "Then neither do I condemn you," Jesus declared. "Go now and leave your life of sin" (John 8:10-11).

THE CHANGE PRINCIPLE

In our continuing study of followology, we come to the **Change Principle**. Looking back, you can probably see a progression similar to the time line in a previous Chat Room. Unnamed needs motivate us to seek answers to spiritual questions. When challenged to follow a person who promises to answer those questions, we choose whether we will follow. If we choose to follow, we will continue to follow if we remain focused. Along the way we build significant relationships with other followers, as well as with the leader. The spiritual application is probably obvious, so this little review is unnecessary. Stay with me, though. If you can trace the first five principles as mile markers in your journey of discipleship, you are changed. Maybe the change was radical and instantaneous. Maybe you haven't noticed it as it has taken place over time, but you are changed. *Christianity emphasizes the incredible power God unlocks in our lives when we choose to follow Jesus.*

> **Christianity emphasizes the incredible power God unlocks in our lives when we choose to follow Jesus.**

▲Chat Room▲▲▲▲▲▲▲▲▲▲▲▲▲▲

Remembering your journey of following, recall when and how the following took place:

Realization of your spiritual need

Choice to follow Jesus

Challenges to staying focused

Evidence of the developing relationship

Noticeable changes that have taken place in your life

▲▲▲▲▲▲▲▲▲▲▲▲▲▲▲▲▲▲▲▲▲▲

Keep the Change

As followologists seeking to become better followers of Jesus, the "change" stories inspire and instruct us. The Scriptures tell about persons who were changed instantly, as well as those who gradually became more like Jesus, their Leader. You have seen such transformation among students at your school. As followology majors, we can observe both types of change in the lives of the disciples.

Anyone who knew Peter, James, John, Andrew, Matthew, and the rest must have marveled at the observable differences in their lives. Matthew was perhaps the most radical of the bunch. We have already looked at his conversion, but the verses are worth repeating to view through the lens of dramatic transformation:

> After this, Jesus went out and saw a tax collector by the name of Levi sitting at his tax booth. "Follow me," Jesus said to him, and Levi got up, left everything and followed him. Then Levi held a great banquet for Jesus at his house, and a large crowd of tax collectors

CHAPTER SEVEN

and others were eating with them. But the Pharisees and the teachers of the law who belonged to their sect complained to his disciples, "Why do you eat and drink with tax collectors and 'sinners'?" Jesus answered them, "It is not the healthy who need a doctor, but the sick" (Luke 5:27-31).

During the three years these men (and others) followed Jesus, they were not aware of the soul surgery taking place. Their initial response to His invitation indicated spiritual interest, but we still aren't sure their early motives were not driven by self-interests rather than by kingdom goals. Yet, they followed. Little did they know the future of Christianity rested on them. John Kramp put it in perspective:

> Frankly, I'm glad they didn't [understand Jesus' mission]. I'm thankful for every one of their struggles. Every time their faith failed, I take heart. Every time they bickered and jockeyed for position, I take comfort. When they could not understand spiritual truths that should have been clear, I grin. And when they fail miserably at the critical moment when Jesus needed their support the most, I sigh with relief. Why? Because all these things convince me that they are just like me, like us.[1]

The "After" Part of "Before and After"

The stories of the twelve in Matthew, Mark, Luke, and John are the "before" shots. If this were a weight loss advertisement, these would be the overweight apostles who were going to do something about it. We have already discovered the obvious—none of these guys was a superhero, nor were many of the other disciples who followed Jesus. To appreciate the changes that took place in the lives of the twelve over time, we must connect their stories in the Gospels with accounts of their role in the early church as found in the Book of Acts. Given the diversity and ordinariness of the disciples, it is amazing to read of the extraordinary things that God did through them in the first-century church.

I told you earlier about Free Speech Alley at LSU. Well, Peter and John were on stage in the first-century equivalent of the Alley, dragged before the same religious leaders who had intimidated them when Jesus was crucified. There, they seemed very different from the trembling disciples who slept through the prayer meeting and then ran for their lives in the Garden of Gethsemane.

> When they saw the courage of Peter and John and realized that they were unschooled, ordinary men, they were astonished and they took note that these men had been with Jesus. But since they could see the man who had been healed standing there with them, there was nothing they could say. So they ordered them to withdraw from the Sanhedrin and then conferred together. "What are we going to do with these men?" they asked. "Everybody living in Jerusalem knows they have done an outstanding miracle, and we cannot deny it. But to stop this thing from spreading any further among the people, we must warn these men to speak no longer to

anyone in this name." Then they called them in again and commanded them not to speak or teach at all in the name of Jesus. But Peter and John replied, "Judge for yourselves whether it is right in God's sight to obey you rather than God. For we cannot help speaking about what we have seen and heard" (Acts 4:13-20).

Allen's paraphrase: "Give it your best shot, guys. We really don't have a choice in the matter, because we have been transformed from the inside out. We got off to a slow start, but we have to make up for lost time!" The passage above was what happened immediately after Peter had roasted the religious establishment by accusing them of crucifying the promised Messiah. At issue was a man who had been healed. The pious elders and teachers of the Law probably had a distant memory of another who had been healed. Jesus had once healed a blind man who gave a simple description of the change in his life:

> Give it your best shot, guys. We really don't have a choice in the matter.

He replied, "Whether he is a sinner or not, I don't know. One thing I do know. I was blind but now I see!" Then they asked him, "What did he do to you? How did he open your eyes?" He answered, "I have told you already and you did not listen. Why do you want to hear it again? Do you want to become his disciples, too?" (John 9:25-27).

The blind man's simple testimony of change reminds me of a sign that supposedly hung in a church in the Old West:

> I ain't what I'm supposed to be,
> I ain't what I'm gonna be,
> But thank God, I ain't what I was.

▲Chat Room▲▲▲▲▲▲▲▲▲▲▲▲▲▲

Which of the following make you think of change? [Circle your answer(s).]

(a) A caterpillar turning into a butterfly

(b) Winter giving way to spring

(c) A new baby is born into a family

(d) You return to a city where you used to live and don't recognize anything

True or False? Put a "T" beside the true and an "F" beside the false.

(a) Change that takes the longest is lasting change.

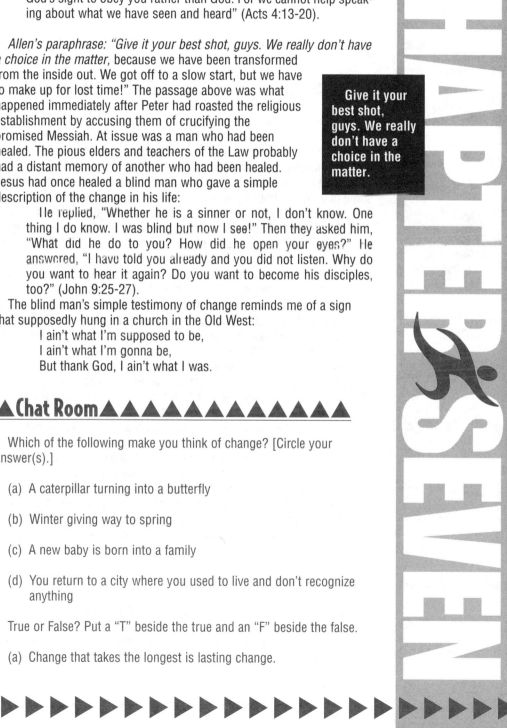

CHAPTER SEVEN

(b) Rapid change is not real change.

(c) Change that is not visible is not real change.

(d) Motivation for change always comes from inside a person.

(e) If we change to please someone else, the change will not last.

▲▲▲▲▲▲▲▲▲▲▲▲▲▲▲▲▲▲▲▲

Good News: Anyone Can Change

People wonder if they can become something other than what they are. The aimlessness of many of the people around you at college is evidence that they are open to a change in their lives. Some of them (and some of you) feel trapped by expectations, confused about the future, and manipulated by social forces. Kevin Ford, in his book, *Jesus for a New Generation*, told stories of Generation Xers who had been changed by Jesus. One sentence speaks of the openness of a generation to such change:

> To an empty postmodern generation we bring the story of One who fills the holes in our souls and who opens the door to transcendent, supernatural realities. To a generation that has lost its sense of direction, that has lost its belief in objective truth, that has become drenched in death and mourning, we bring the story of the way, the truth and the life.[2]

In contrast to the self-help remedies, psychic friends, and bogus prophets, Jesus offers hope for real change. Paul phrased it simply enough: "Therefore, if anyone is in Christ, he is a new creation; the old has gone, the new has come!" (2 Cor. 5:17).

SPIRITUAL GROWTH

We follow Jesus because He changes us. As we follow, the Leader touches our lives and slowly makes us what we dreamed we could be and what He intended for us to be all along. The process can be slow and costly. Just ask Jesus. He took a group of ordinary people and took them step by step through the process that eventually brought them from "before" to "after." Sometimes, however, we run into another barrier in the process. Brandon, in our story, ran into that barrier. It is named "failure."

Those Who Fail Can Follow Again

There is a web page on the Internet that features stories of people who have attempted to be criminals, but aren't very good at it. At the risk of calling in the political correctness authorities, I simply repeat the terminology used on the net: "Stupid Criminal Stories." Here are a few for your enjoyment:[3]

▶▶▶▶▶   ▶▶▶▶▶▶▶▶▶▶▶▶▶▶▶▶▶

Police in Vero Beach, FL, raided the home of a suspected drug dealer after he took the wrong bag to the cleaners. David Snyder, 37, delivered what he thought was a sack of dirty clothes to a local laundry, but a worker there found three lbs. of marijuana in the bag instead.

A man in Johannesburg, South Africa, was charged with shooting his 49-year-old friend in the face, seriously wounding him, while the two practiced shooting beer cans off each other's head.

A man in Seattle, WA, attempted to steal gasoline out of a motor home by siphoning it through a hose. He put the hose in the sewage tank instead, and police found a very, very sick would-be thief, curled up on the ground.

Disguised in camouflage and with a rag tied around his face, a man in Springfield, TN, broke into his own grandparents' home and started beating them in an attempt to rob them. Grandma put a stop to his antics by hitting him upside the head with a flatiron.

Even Michael Failed!

Michael Jordan was voted the Most Valuable Player at the 1998 NBA All Star Game after scoring a game-high 23 points, leading the East team to victory. It was the third MVP for the 34-year-old NBA veteran who said it was his last All Star game. Jordan is in the twilight of his career in which he has established himself as one of the greatest basketball players of all time. Under his leadership, the Chicago Bulls have won five NBA titles. But as a sophomore, Michael Jordan was cut from his high school basketball team!

We Fail, Too

I don't know if you have ever failed at anything major. I told you I couldn't juggle like my brother. I have failed in some other ways as well, but the most devastating failure I have ever been through was at a time when God was trying to get my attention to call me into full-time student ministry. I had just graduated college with a degree in business administration, with high hopes of entering the job market in a lucrative, if entry level, position in a medium-sized corporation. God had other plans, but I ignored the still, small voice saying that ministry was where I would find vocational meaning. The short version of the story is that I interviewed for nine months without a single offer. My confidence hit rock bottom, and I *finally* listened to that voice and continued my education at seminary.

▲Chat Room▲▲▲▲▲▲▲▲▲▲▲▲

Here are some reasons why we fail as we try to follow. Put a check beside each one that represents an experience you would be willing to

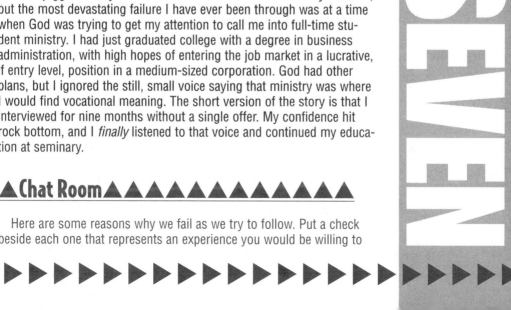

share. If you are working through this book alone, put your thoughts in the journal entry below.

❏ Fear   ❏ Ambition   ❏ Disappointment
❏ Time management   ❏ Addictions   ❏ Profanity
❏ The past   ❏ Habitual sin   ❏ Anger
❏ Family relationships

In the space below, write a few words to describe to God how you felt in the face of your failure.

▲▲▲▲▲▲▲▲▲▲▲▲▲▲▲▲▲▲▲

All of Jesus' followers failed, as did other biblical characters like David, Saul, Noah, and Moses. None failed as miserably as did Simon Peter. He tried to walk on water—fish food. He tried to defend Jesus in the Garden—soldier minus an ear. He tried to stay awake during Jesus' agonizing prayer—attacked by the sandman. In his defense, Peter was always trying to follow Jesus more closely. His greatest and most memorable failure is the one Jesus predicted in Luke 22:31. Simon Peter denied that he even knew Jesus. So how did he get from the *before* of change to the *after?* Read on.

Between the "Before" and the "After"

Many sermons have been preached on the transformation that took place in Simon Peter's life between the denials during the mockery that was Jesus' trial and the powerful preacher of Acts 4. The inescapable fact is that he had to bounce back from a failure of epic proportions even by today's standards. His failure is almost as widely known as that of David, a man after God's own heart, but also after Uriah's own wife.

It is helpful to trace the biblical account of what Peter did between his failure and his magnificent pulpit performance. Work through some Scripture:

1. *Examine, he remembered the words of Jesus.*
   The Lord turned and looked straight at Peter. Then Peter remembered the word the Lord had spoken to him: "Before the rooster crows today, you will disown me three times" (Luke 22:61).

Peter could have come down with a case of selected amnesia, beaten himself up over the guilt of turning his back on his friend, and walked away. He was spiritually changed, though, and he couldn't help but remember what Jesus had said. I don't know how many of Jesus' words he remembered. Maybe he only remembered the words that predicted the denials. Maybe he remembered the words where Jesus promised that Peter would come through his failure and become a foundational stone in the church. Jesus has left us many words to remember, too.

2. *See, he wept tears of repentance over his failure.*
> And he went outside and wept bitterly (Luke 22:62).

There is a difference between tears of repentance and tears of, "I'm sorry I got caught." The tears here seem to be shed out of genuine sorrow for the sin and the potentially devastating consequences. Even more, Peter wept at the canyon that had opened up in his relationship with Jesus. The later verses tell us that Peter was sorry enough to deal with his sin and allow Jesus to continue to change him. That is repentance. I am sad to admit that I cannot remember very many times that I have wept bitter tears over a spiritual failure in my life. Like Thomas, I have doubted. Like the others, I have run from association with my Christianity. Like Peter, I have denied Jesus. But where are the tears?

3. *Notice, he continued to pursue Jesus.*
> Early on the first day of the week, while it was still dark, Mary Magdalene went to the tomb and saw that the stone had been removed from the entrance. So she came running to Simon Peter and the other disciple, the one Jesus loved, and said, "They have taken the Lord out of the tomb, and we don't know where they have put him!" So Peter and the other disciple started for the tomb. Both were running, but the other disciple outran Peter and reached the tomb first (John 20:1-4).

I think it would have been pretty easy for Peter to conclude that the whole three years with Jesus had been a trip to Fantasy Island. I also wonder what he thought when he first heard that Jesus was alive. Was he at all ashamed, anticipating that Jesus would remind him of his failure? Did he hesitate, fearing that he wouldn't be welcomed back as Jesus' friend? Apparently not. In the face of his failure, he rushed back to Jesus. The relationship with the Leader overshadowed the failure.

4. *Observe, he stayed quiet as he grieved over his sin.*
> Read John 20—pretty much all of it!

An argument from silence. Turn there now and see if you can find anything Peter said. Nothing. I don't find many other places when Jesus was speaking to the disciples and Peter didn't have anything to say. He was the leader among the other followers, the talkative one. He often spoke before he had something to say, and it sometimes got him into trouble. Yet here, he is noticeably quiet. I think he was still brooding. Even after he saw Jesus at the tomb, the Bible does not record that Peter had much to say. No quotes are ascribed to him in John 20. Not until John 21 do we see that the cat turns loose of Peter's tongue. Then he has a conversation with Jesus in which you can see the restoration of a failure.

5. *Finally, he stayed in fellowship with other believers.*
> Simon Peter, Thomas (called Didymus), Nathanael from Cana in Galilee, the sons of Zebedee, and two other disciples were together (John 21:2).

CHAPTER SEVEN

When I have messed up and everyone knows about it, I am not all that anxious to be around the previously mentioned "everyone." I arrogantly predicted the winner of the Super Bowl in front of a youth group where I was interim minister of youth. I was glad the new youth minister came to the church right after the Super Bowl was played and I was proved gloriously wrong, because I really didn't want to catch the flak for my errant prognostication (that means I messed up). Peter could have felt like he didn't want to be around the 10 men who reminded him the most of his failure. But the Bible records that he stayed with them.

▲Chat Room▲▲▲▲▲▲▲▲▲▲▲▲▲▲

For each of the five things Peter did in the face of failure, write a couple of sentences that would make the spiritual application to your life. If it were you who messed up, and you chose to do the things Peter did, what would it be like? Use first person language.

1. He remembered the words of Jesus.

2. He wept tears of repentance over his failure.

3. He continued to pursue Jesus.

4. He stayed quiet as he grieved over his sin.

5. He stayed in fellowship with other believers.

▲▲▲▲▲▲▲▲▲▲▲▲▲▲▲▲▲▲▲▲▲▲

▶▶▶▶▶ ▶▶▶▶▶▶▶▶▶▶▶▶▶▶▶▶▶

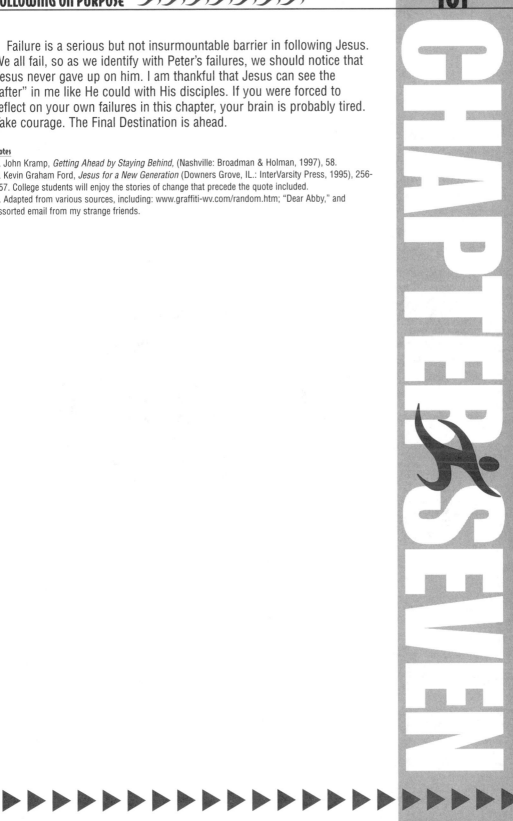

Failure is a serious but not insurmountable barrier in following Jesus. We all fail, so as we identify with Peter's failures, we should notice that Jesus never gave up on him. I am thankful that Jesus can see the "after" in me like He could with His disciples. If you were forced to reflect on your own failures in this chapter, your brain is probably tired. Take courage. The Final Destination is ahead.

Notes
1. John Kramp, *Getting Ahead by Staying Behind,* (Nashville: Broadman & Holman, 1997), 58.
2. Kevin Graham Ford, *Jesus for a New Generation* (Downers Grove, IL.: InterVarsity Press, 1995), 256-257. College students will enjoy the stories of change that precede the quote included.
3. Adapted from various sources, including: www.graffiti-wv.com/random.htm; "Dear Abby," and assorted email from my strange friends.

CHAPTER SEVEN

CHAPTER SEVEN

YOU'RE FOLLOWING ON PURPOSE!

C H A P T E R   E I G H T

FOLLOWING ALL THE WAY HOME

Followology Principle: *The Destination Principle emphasizes the reward of following.*
Followology Barrier: *Reluctant Leadership (People sometimes resist becoming a follower of leaders.)*

Mitch didn't even try to seek treatment for her near-terminal case of "senioritis." Graduation day was finally on *this month's* calendar. Over 130 semester hours were in the registrar's computer in her name, the last year-and-a-half of which were in her major. Library books had been turned in, parking tickets had been paid, cap and gown had been ordered. The diploma, representing a degree in marine biology, would read "Teresa Michelle," but all anyone had ever called her was Mitch.

She was told her dad had started it. Rumor had it that he really wanted a boy, and that explained why she could play volleyball with the best of the boys, hold her own with a fishing pole, and even change the oil in her own car. She was especially fond of the fishing trips when she and her father would go out in the little boat to find hungry catfish. Her dad had taught her how to do many "guy things," but she was far from a tomboy.

Uncle Randy had suggested that she apply to join him at the institute when she completed her undergraduate degree. In a real way, she had followed Randy for most of her life. He was only seven years older than Mitch, her dad being the oldest child among his siblings.

Her admiration for Randy and his cause was a motivating factor that seemed to point her back to marine biology. Her favorite uncle (who was more like a big brother) finally convinced her she needed to surrender to her real love and head out to sea. Randy had been a lot of help along the way. He had placed a few strategic phone calls as she applied for scholarships to help with university tuition. He had coached her on major assignments, suggesting research topics significant in the field.

More than following Uncle Randy as a marine biologist, Mitch had followed him as a Christian who happened to be involved in science. She was afraid at first, having heard stories of how scientific types automatically fell away from their faith. After all, science and religion were not compatible. If you believed in the supernatural, you were too biased to make a good scientist. So she had heard and wondered if she were a strong enough Christian. Such was the topic of many conversations with her mentor, uncle, and friend.

Randy, however, saw his interest in marine life as an expression of awe for the magnificent creation God had given humans. He considered it an act of stewardship to be the best marine biologist he could be. Someone had to care for the creatures of the planet. He often told of his belief that God had entrusted Adam with the task of caring for the animals on the earth. Randy saw his career as a way that he could carry on that task. Each new species discovered, or each endangered animal saved, was a way he could serve God with his talents and abilities.

Somewhere around her junior year in high school, Mitch had begun to embrace Randy's theology. She could serve God through serving the marine animal kingdom. So she had majored in marine bio, interned at Sea World, and was slated to head to the coast to start a career. The destination was in sight. Her Bible study leader on campus had observed that Mitch's journey almost had a spiritual feel to it. She had chosen to follow a particular path toward the goal of a job in her field. She had disciplined herself to stay concentrated, acquiring the necessary knowledge and tools to be proficient. She had come through the doubts and uncertainties, adjusting her expectations along the way. She had built relationships with other marine biology students, even introducing some of them to her increasingly well-known uncle. She had changed from a carefree freshman to a focused senior, ready to zero in on her dreams. Yes, the destination was in sight.

An unexpected wrinkle had come up Mitch's final semester at college. She had agreed to lead a Bible study of freshman girls. They were a great bunch, often reminding her of her own first year at school. They asked a million questions, made "freshman mistakes," and at times seemed to be too naïve to survive. As Mitch prepared to graduate, she turned the leadership of the Bible study over to one of the girls. When she met with Judi about taking on the role of teacher, the younger girl made a remark that startled her. Judi told her, "Mitch, I want to be like you." Mitch had always viewed Randy as her role model, both vocationally and spiritually. It didn't occur to her that someone would be following her. Judi was a bright student, possibly a marine biology major, and had a sweet Christian spirit. Mitch was so wrapped up in preparing for the move to the institute that she didn't see how much Judi had patterned her life after her Bible study leader. It seemed ironic that Mitch was the one being followed for a change. She wasn't sure how she felt about it.

The Destination Principle

Followism #11 states that, *"Followers go where their leaders are going."* Physically, you can grasp this truth. For example, if you see someone you know in the mall, but they don't see you—and you want to talk to them—they become your leader. You try to catch them as they work their way through the mall. You think they went into Sears or maybe Eddie Bauer, or maybe the Gap. At any rate, you see glimpses of them every now and then. Their agenda becomes your agenda, and where they end up, you will end up—if you are a good follower! In your mind is the question, Where are they going? How can you get where they are going?

> Followers go where their leaders are going.

Notice the subtle progression from other principles to the destination principle. When you choose a leader, you may not initially be overly concerned about the ultimate destination. You find a quality person to follow, and you go where he or she goes. You were motivated by a need to go somewhere besides where you were, and you paid attention to make sure to stay close. Along the way, you built a relationship with that leader. You figure that this is a worthwhile journey. You begin to be changed, becoming more like your leader. Somewhere among the things that go bump in the night, you realize that wherever the leader ends up, you will end up in the same place. In Chapter Two, I told you my fraternity story. If after I had been in the fraternity for awhile, I noticed that most of the leaders in the frat were either failing out of school or in jail for various reasons, I might conclude that the destination of the fraternity was not one I desired for myself. When we are following, we will end up where our leader ends up.

Faithful following yields the reward of a destination reached. The final destination for Christians is heaven. The destination does not take anything away from the joy of the journey or the experiences encountered along the way. Heaven as a destination for Phase Two followers does provide the icing on the cake. Paul understood the importance of the destination:

> For what I received I passed on to you as of first importance: that Christ died for our sins according to the Scriptures, that he was buried, that he was raised on the third day according to the Scriptures, and that he appeared to Peter, and then to the Twelve. After that, he appeared to more than five hundred of the brothers at the same time, most of whom are still living, though some have fallen asleep. Then he appeared to James, then to all the apostles (1 Cor. 15:3-7).

That Jesus returned from the dead establishes the fact of eternal life. While aware of the abundant life that following Jesus yields, Paul nevertheless declared that if the leader weren't going somewhere special, we as followers were just taking a walk:

> But if it is preached that Christ has been raised from the dead, how can some of you say that there is no resurrection of the dead? If there is no resurrection of the dead, then not even Christ has been raised. And if Christ has not been raised, our preaching is useless and so is your faith (1 Cor. 15:12-14).

▲Chat Room▲▲▲▲▲▲▲▲▲▲▲▲▲

Our final destination as Christians is heaven. Beginning with the letter A and going as far as you can through the alphabet, write a word that describes what you think HEAVEN will be like.

A_____ N_____
B_____ O_____
C_____ P_____
D_____ Q_____
E_____ R_____
F_____ S_____
G_____ T_____
H_____ U_____
I_____ V_____
J_____ W_____
K_____ X_____
L_____ Y_____
M_____ Z_____

Without checking the Bible first, list one thing you can think of that Jesus said about heaven.

1.

A Destination to Come

It is not surprising that Jesus had so much to say about the spiritual destination or reward for following Him. On the last night He was alive, several memorable events took place. Before serving the Passover meal, He washed His disciples' feet. He warned that there was a betrayer among them (like us, each disciple had to admit that he could be that betrayer). He told Peter that before sunrise he would deny that he even knew the Master. And He told them about a place beyond their present troubles:

"Do not let your hearts be troubled. Trust in God; trust also in me. In my Father's house are many rooms; if it were not so, I would have told you. I am going there to prepare a place for you. And if I go and prepare a place for you, I will come back and take you to be with me that you also may be where I am. You know the way to the place where I am going" (John 14:1-4).

Considerable unrest erupted among the twelve. Have you ever been told by a close friend that he or she was moving away? Perhaps you have recently been told by someone you care about that they were transferring to another school. In spite of promises to keep in touch, it remains to be seen whether that will actually happen. One of my closest friends here at the seminary announced this week that he was resigning from his faculty and administrative position to become the president at another university. While I am elated at his opportunity, I still have a sick feeling in my stomach that signals a friend is going away. And I cannot go with him.

Jesus was going to a place where the disciples could not go—at least for now. They could not grasp that their leader was moving farther ahead of them so that He could prepare the destination for their eventual arrival. Followers always share the destination with their leaders. They weren't convinced *or* comforted. Where was this place? How did one get there? Why couldn't they go now? What was it like? Jesus described it in terms they could understand.

▲Chat Room▲▲▲▲▲▲▲▲▲▲▲▲▲

Try a matching exercise to remember the description of heaven that Jesus gave us:

___ 1. Matthew 6:20

(a) There, all the world's people, from east and west would join in a feast with Abraham, Isaac, and Jacob

___ 2. Matthew 8:11

(b) The destination would have incalculable value—like a treasure hidden in a field or a pearl of great price.

_____ 3. Matthew 13:31,33

(c) Their destination would be a wonderful place where spiritual treasures would be stored and never destroyed.

_____ 4. Matthew 13:44-45

(d) The place He prepared could be found easily with a child's faith while remaining invisible to proud eyes.

_____ 5. Matthew 18:3-4

(e) The place He prepared for them would exceed all expectations, like the growth of a mustard seed or the work of yeast in dough.

The answers are c-a-e-b-d.

▲▲▲▲▲▲▲▲▲▲▲▲▲▲▲▲▲▲▲▲▲▲

But We Want to Come Now

Jesus tried to help His disciples understand the complicated mystery that is the atonement. Before they could all be together in the wonderful place that David had described, Jesus had to die and defeat death. Each of the disciples would have eventful lives before they arrived at the destination to be shared with Jesus. He tried to help them comprehend the preparations He would make for them, but they struggled to understand. Thomas thought he would voice the common concern of the disciples: Thomas said to him, "Lord, we don't know where you are going, so how can we know the way?" (John 14:5).

Jesus answered that He was the Way. Their leader was the only way to the destination, and it was not enough for Him simply to draw a map. They would have to keep on following. They were comforted but not yet convinced. If they kept Him in sight, they would reach the destination. As Phase One followers, they couldn't begin to understand that their following would have to move into a different dimension—Phase Two. The writer of Hebrews encouraged Phase Two followers with these words:

CROSS
SEEKERS

Therefore, since we are surrounded by such a great cloud of witnesses, let us throw off everything that hinders and the sin that so easily entangles, and let us run with perseverance the race marked out for us. Let us fix our eyes on Jesus, the author and perfecter of our faith, who for the joy set before him endured the cross, scorning its shame, and sat down at the right hand of the throne of God. Consider him who endured such opposition from sinful men, so that you will not grow weary and lose heart (Heb. 12:1-3).

Fixing Our Eyes on Jesus

As college students, you will face days of uncertainty. You anxiously wait on a grade, your roommate moves into a sorority house, your financial aid application is rejected. When we are beaten up, we must fix our spiritual eyes on Jesus, our Leader who endured a cross on the way to His final destination. That same destination awaits us—prepared by the One we follow. Yet as followers, we want to know more. Years ago, a woman wrote to Billy Graham to inquire about heaven. Her letter was published in his weekly column.

> Dear Dr. Graham: What will we look like in heaven? To be honest, I've always wanted to be a lot more beautiful than I really am and I wondered if maybe I would be beautiful in heaven. Or will we be just spirits wandering around without bodies?[1]

Dr. Graham answered her letter,

> No, we will not just be "spirits wandering around." God will give us new bodies—bodies that will never experience pain or decay or sickness, because they will be like the body Jesus was given after His resurrection. "Listen, I tell you a mystery: We will not all sleep, but we will all be changed—in a flash, in the twinkling of an eye, at the last trumpet. For the trumpet will sound, the dead will be raised imperishable, and we will be changed. For the perishable must clothe itself with the imperishable, and the mortal with immortality." (1 Cor. 15:51-53).[2]

In 1988, *Newsweek* commissioned a Gallup poll to find out what people thought about heaven.
- 91% think it will be peaceful
- 83% think they will be with God
- 77% think they will see people they know
- 74% think there will be humor
- 32% think they'll be the same age in heaven as when they die on earth[3]

Heavenly Minds, but Earthly Bodies

For all of eternity we will continue to enjoy our relationship with Him—a relationship begun as we follow here on earth. In heaven, we will be changed fully into His image as Dr. Graham told his writer. Following Jesus on earth is part of that transformation process. Whatever heaven is, Jesus will be at the center of it. It is His house, and we are the invited guests. We have been asked to follow Him home.

CHAPTER EIGHT

CHAPTER EIGHT

▲ Chat Room ▲▲▲▲▲▲▲▲▲▲▲▲▲

Does a long trip take on a new feeling when you consider the destination? Check one.

❑ Yes ❑ No ❑ Maybe ❑ Don't know

In what ways does the reality of heaven impact the way you live now? Explain as briefly as possible.

▲▲▲▲▲▲▲▲▲▲▲▲▲▲▲▲▲▲▲

Even with the Wrong Leader, We Still Reach the Leader's Destination

Of course, the following process works the same way if we follow the wrong leader. If we choose an evil leader, we still end up where that leader is going. People centered in the pleasures of the flesh have destinations other than the one we have described, and their followers go along with them. Jim Jones was the leader of a cult in Guyana who ordered a mass suicide in November of 1978. Over nine hundred members of his flock followed him to death by drinking a beverage laced with cyanide. The writer of Proverbs counseled against such foolishness: "There is a way that seems right to a man, but in the end it leads to death" (Prov. 14:12).

Whether we become wise followers or foolish followers, we will reach a destination. There we will find our reward, the sum total of the choices we have made along the way. But wait, there may be someone behind you!

A FINAL BARRIER: RELUCTANCE TO BECOME A LEADER OF FOLLOWERS

A comedian is making a living these days telling jokes that begin with "You might be a redneck if . . ." Hundreds of other lists have been inspired, so I decided to give you my attempt.

You might be a leader of followers if . . .

- your identity as a Christian has ever been questioned because you made a mistake.
- you have ever not been invited to a party because you don't party.
- you understand that eternity is a long time, and that heaven is the best place to spend it.
- you think you might be here for a reason.

• you think your part of that reason might be to help others as they learn to follow.

Most people do not think of themselves as leaders. Yet as followologists, we accept that some people will follow us. Perhaps someone in the dorm or apartment is watching us to see if we are authentic. If they decide that we are, even without knowing it, we become a leader of followers. In most cases, our role of leadership will be informal rather than structured. Either way, our assignment is simply stated: *Follow me, as I follow Christ.* Paul said in 1 Corinthians 4:16, "Therefore I urge you to imitate me." Pretty bold statement. The complement to that verse is found in 1 Corinthians 11:1: "Follow my example, as I follow the example of Christ." Again in Ephesians 5:1: "Be imitators of God, therefore, as dearly loved children." Paul understood his role as a leader of followers.

▲Chat Room▲ ▲ ▲ ▲ ▲ ▲ ▲ ▲ ▲ ▲ ▲

Look up in the Bible each of the Scripture passages listed. Write a sentence for each of the following verses, but structure the sentences like a job description.

The duties of a leader of followers shall include the following:

John 13:15

1 Corinthians 10:11

1 Timothy 4:12

1 Peter 2:21

1 Peter 5:3

Each of the accounts of Jesus' life that we call the Gospels has a final instruction to the disciples: multiply. Remember the skit I told you about in which an angel asked Jesus about Plan B, and Jesus responded that there was no other plan? Find the instruction in each of the following verses:

Matthew 28:18-20

John 21:15-17 (He said it three times!)

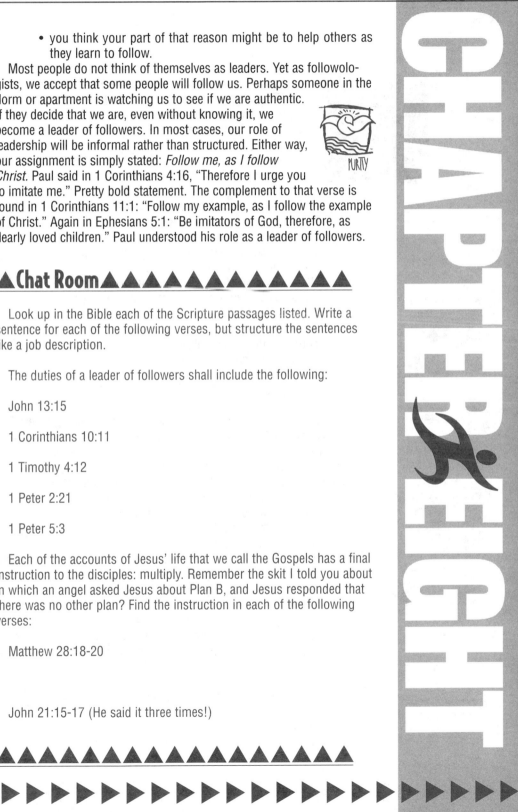

CHAPTER EIGHT

One of the reasons we might be reluctant is because we don't feel worthy. John Kramp helped us see more clearly that our worthiness to be a leader of followers is not the issue. *Our closeness to Jesus as a follower is what qualifies us to be a leader.* Jesus knows the way, and if we stay close to Him, it is okay for others to stay close to us. What we do as disciples is different from any other type of leadership.[4]

> **Our closeness to Jesus as a follower is what qualifies us to be a leader.**

- Our first responsibility as Christians is to follow Christ. If we are not doing that, we have nothing of value to offer other people.
- If we are following Christ, other people can learn more about following Jesus as they follow us.
- We need to help people focus on following Jesus. HE must become their ultimate leader. Our goal is to get out of the way, so they have a clear view of Jesus.
- We cannot lead others to follow Jesus further than we have followed Him ourselves. We can't lead people where we haven't been with Jesus.
- If we stop following Jesus for whatever reason, we must discourage others from following us. It is dangerous to lead others when we don't know the way.

The Challenge of Being Followed

I tell college students all the time, "Everybody is somebody's hero." We are leaders whether we are speaking to thousands or nurturing one disciple. We can overcome our reluctance to being a leader of followers when we understand that it is natural, expected, and accomplished with the help of the Holy Spirit. For the strength to be a leader, there are some truths that should help keep the fuel in our tank:

- Whatever the price, spend time alone with God. Time to be still, to think. Jesus did it often, so we should take time to refresh our relationship with Him.
- We need to take time to renew our minds through reading, memorizing, and meditating on the Scriptures. Challenge yourself to engage in some personal Bible study even when you aren't preparing to teach.
- Pray regularly and systematically. Keep a prayer journal to see God work through those whom He has allowed you to lead.
- In addition to the spiritual, exercise physically and rest regularly. Our bodies need to stay up to the task as well.

▲Chat Room▲▲▲▲▲▲▲▲▲▲▲▲▲

Can you measure where you need to prepare to be a leader of followers? Answer each of the questions in your mind. . .and be honest!

What has God called you to do?

What do you want to do?

What can you do that others cannot or will not do?

What do you want more of in your life?

What do you want less of in your life?

▲▲▲▲▲▲▲▲▲▲▲▲▲▲▲▲▲▲▲▲ ▲

Living a Legacy

We can thank God for those who allowed us to follow them. They loved us even when we interrupted. When we called, demanding atten- tion, they invited us to come over. When we were selfish, they chal- lenged us to higher standards. When we rebelled and walked away, they nurtured a dream for our future and expected us to fulfill it. Many invested in us so that we can invest in others. As hard as it is to envi- sion, those who follow you as you follow Jesus will have followers one day (if they don't already).

▲Chat Room▲▲▲▲▲▲▲▲▲▲▲▲ ▲

Take a few moments to write a thank you note to one of the people who discipled you. Send it tomorrow.

Draw a "family tree" of followers. Place Jesus as the Leader, and those who followed followers in line, leading up to you. If anyone is fol- lowing you, include their names as well. Then take a moment to pray for the whole list.

Jesus

▲▲▲▲▲▲▲▲▲▲▲▲▲▲▲▲▲▲▲▲▲

▶ ▶ ▶ ▶ ▶ ▶ ▶ ▶ ▶ ▶ ▶ ▶ ▶ ▶ ▶ ▶▶▶▶

CHAPTER EIGHT

A Final Analysis: The Difference You Can Make

When I was a pledge trainer in the fraternity, the movie *Animal House* had just been released. One of the scenes in the fraternity showed rush parties where guys who weren't "fraternity material" were shuffled off to sit with other "geeks" who wouldn't become Greeks (until, of course, they found the infamous Delta House). Some aspects of that scene were a little too real. After I graduated and was in youth ministry, I found this story. I wish I would have had it to read to the pledges in my care. I would have used it to read to the pledge classes to let them know what it really means to care for people.

The boy's name was Jon. He was a bright kid. He came to the University in the autumn of 1968 for his freshman year, and he signed up for fraternity rush. There was something wrong with him that made him look unusual. He wasn't crippled, but his stride was unusual. Maybe he didn't know what was ahead for him, and maybe he did, but he determined to do his best.

His best wasn't very good. At the first house where he showed up for a rush party, one of the brothers saw him and grinned. He made an easy target, and he was placed in a corner by himself. No one greeted him, no one spoke, and when the other rushees were taken to the dining room for a meal, Jon was left alone. When the other potential pledges came back upstairs to leave, Jon got up and left with them.

The scene was repeated at house after house. Some were subtle, some were not. Sometimes, Jon even had company—others who were not deemed to be "fraternity material." At one house, he was led to a fire escape where he waited for two hours alone. It was an unbelievable cruelty shown towards another human being.

One night, two active brothers of one of the fraternities were assigned to make a rush call in the dorm where Jon lived. By mistake, they ended up in Jon's room. They were seniors, and somewhat tired of the frat system, but when they heard Jon's story, they discovered a new fire to bring about change. He told them what had happened during the first part of rush week. He told them how afraid he was of college and how he just wanted to fit in. They suddenly realized that Jon's story was the story of so many young men that it made them a little sick.

They listened quietly and left the dorm with a resolve to do something about it. They went to the rush office and got Jon's schedule for the rest of the week. That night, they started to visit all the houses where Jon would be going. At every house, they asked to talk to the senior leaders in the fraternity. They explained what they had come for. And they said, "We are not asking you to accept him into your house. We are asking you to treat him with a little decency."

Not surprisingly, there were leaders at every house who had similar feelings. The two seniors weren't sure why they were doing what they were doing. They only knew that it felt right. It was the first time they had gone against the flow for someone else.

Jon went through the rest of rush week. He was not asked to join a fraternity, but he was treated with a measure of respect. The seniors in all of the houses saw to it that someone ate with him, talked with him, and made him feel welcome. Maybe Jon's pain was lessened a little.

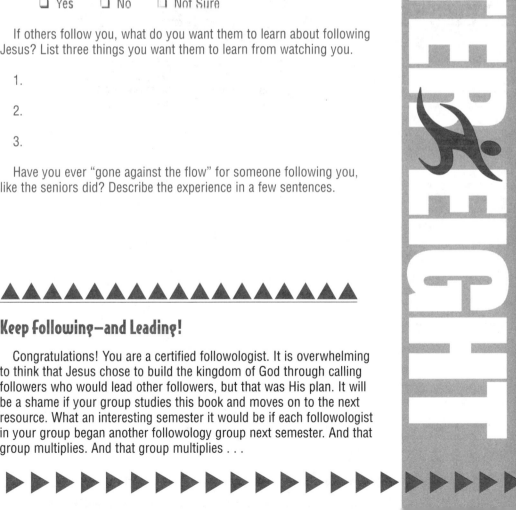

WITNESS

The two seniors graduated the following spring. Like many seniors in the Greek system, they were less involved than they had been. Maybe they were disillusioned, and maybe they were just tired. But maybe they made a difference in the attitudes of some of the younger members. They didn't know if they had made a difference in Jon's life or not.

On the day of graduation, a congratulatory card came to their apartment in the mail. It was from Jon. "Thank you. . ." it said.[5]

▲ Chat Room ▲▲▲▲▲▲▲▲▲▲▲▲▲

Do you think of yourself as a leader? Check one.

❏ Yes   ❏ No   ❏ Not Sure

If others follow you, what do you want them to learn about following Jesus? List three things you want them to learn from watching you.

1.

2.

3.

Have you ever "gone against the flow" for someone following you, like the seniors did? Describe the experience in a few sentences.

▲▲▲▲▲▲▲▲▲▲▲▲▲▲▲▲▲▲▲▲▲▲▲

Keep Following—and Leading!

Congratulations! You are a certified followologist. It is overwhelming to think that Jesus chose to build the kingdom of God through calling followers who would lead other followers, but that was His plan. It will be a shame if your group studies this book and moves on to the next resource. What an interesting semester it would be if each followologist in your group began another followology group next semester. And that group multiplies. And that group multiplies . . .

▶▶▶▶▶▶▶▶▶▶▶▶▶▶▶▶▶▶▶

CHAPTER EIGHT

CHAPTER EIGHT

Notes

1. "Believers Will Receive New Bodies in Heaven" *The Town Talk* (Alexandria, Louisiana), March 15, 1987.

2. Ibid.

3. "Heaven," *Newsweek*, March 27, 1989, 53. The poll was a national sample of 750 adults by telephone, Dec. 21-22, 1988.

4. John Kramp, *Getting Ahead by Staying Behind,* (Nashville, Broadman & Holman, 1997), 157.

5. Adapted from a story found in 1983. Source unknown.

FOLLOWING PAYS OFF!

C O N C L U S I O N

CONGRATS!

You have completed all of the course requirements for *Followology 101-102*. Congratulations. The goal throughout this book has been to ask you to compare spiritual following with physical following. If you were following someone on foot or in a car, what would it take to continue following? What would motivate you to begin following in the first place? How would you determine that a leader is worth following? How do you make sure you turn when she turns, stop when she stops, go when she goes, and ultimately reach *her* destination with her? Along the way, what barriers slow you down, what barriers separate you from your leader? How does one get back to following after temporary setbacks? What happens if I look back and notice people following *me*? The responsibility seems so great!

Application was made from a spiritual point of view. What need in us drives us to choose Jesus as our Leader? Is He one of *many* choices, or is He *the* way, *the* truth, and *the* life? Does it ever get easier to pay attention and remain in His will as we follow? As we are in relationship with Jesus and other followers, our priorities and desires change. Will old friends be left behind? How can we adjust our lives to stay where God is working, where Jesus is leading? The responsibility of being a leader of followers seems great, yet each of the Gospel accounts ends with Jesus telling us to make disciples.

If some of your questions were answered and others gave way to even more questions, then I did my job. As college students, you must think. It is intellectual suicide to simply accept just any teaching or any leader who happens to drift onto your campus. Followologists keep Jesus firmly in their sight. They compare any new teaching to the words He left us in the Bible to live by and to test other teachings against.

Modern day followologists also have the added challenge of following

a Leader we cannot see. Jesus had Phase Two followers in mind when He said to Thomas:

> "Put your finger here; see my hands. Reach out your hand and put it into my side. Stop doubting and believe." Thomas said to him, "My Lord and my God!" Then Jesus told him, "Because you have seen me, you have believed; blessed are those who have not seen and yet have believed" (John 20:27-29).

Followology is meant to be a practical connection. If I have made discipleship less understandable rather than easier to grasp, I have not done well. If you are less challenged to become a followologist than you were before you read this book, then call me, and we will try again. I am absolutely convinced that college students are pivotal in the evangelism of the planet. You come into contact with more people who are young Christians than any other group of people. It is no accident that major revivals and discipleship movements often begin among collegiate students.

As I finished this book, I became aware that the principles of followology could be seen in everyday life. They are not limited to an intentional spiritual application, but emerge in common experiences as well. Look for opportunities on your campus to discover the principles of followology in your experiences.

Thank You

Thank you for letting me share personally with you. I hope that followology will become so popular as a discipline that your university or college will have to begin offering it as a major. Stay close to Jesus! Follow Jesus in the Real World!

CONGRATULATIONS! FOLLOW ON!

Followology Helps

This section is designed to help facilitate individual as well as small group study of followology. As you examine the suggested outline or adapt as necessary for a quality learning experience, hopefully you will become a better "followologist."

Read this book carefully. Teach each of the twenty-four followisms found in the introduction of the book. Although the book will not address them specifically, all twenty-four are found within the contents of the book.

Read *Getting Ahead By Staying Behind* by John Kramp to enhance your study and give greater understanding of following.

If you are leading a group study, advertise the study and the date you plan to begin. Enlist students who are creative and artistic to help with advertising. Copy and place the twenty-four followisms in locations where they can be seen by potential participants.

Order a copy of *Followology @ Collegiate Ministry: Following Jesus In the Real World* for each participant. Distribute books before the first group session. Encourage students to bring their books to the study.

Inform participants the study is for eight weeks. Students who choose to participate should make attendance at each session for the eight weeks a priority. For group study, enlist 8-10 students for optimal group experience.

Secure a quiet room, if possible, where students can share their experiences without interruption from outside elements. Make sure the room is easy to find.

Obtain other equipment you might need. For example, you might develop for group study the twenty-four followisms on overhead cels or put them into a powerpoint presentation. You might also want to develop a powerpoint presentation of the six principles and six barriers or be prepared to have them on large tear sheets to display in the room. These should be prepared before the actual classes begin. Whatever teaching methods are most comfortable for you will be easy to adapt in the group sessions with this material.

Begin praying for an openness to the process of following by those who are leaders in their own right.

FOLLOWOLOGY HIGHLIGHTS

The book has several unique characteristics worth mentioning as we begin.

1. **The case study**–At the beginning of each chapter there is a personal case study. Take time to read the study. It will help you both individually and in a small group setting.

2. **Chat Room**–Throughout the book you will find boxes called "Chat Rooms." These are not simply boxes to fill in the blanks. Rather, they open the door for you to share your thoughts with other students. In many cases, this will be a global experience as you share through a real chat room on the www.crossseekers.org web page. In each case, the Chat Room is designed to give you the opportunity to reflect and think about what you have read and are learning about followology.

3. **CrossSeekers icons**—CrossSeekers is a discipleship movement among college students built on six principles based on Scripture. You will find the CrossSeekers icons explained toward the end of the book. When an icon appears, it is to direct your thinking to covenant living. Look at them carefully within the context of the passage where they are found.

4. **Quotation box**—Within the text you will find "Quotation boxes" which are designed to give you a special thought to think about. The quote is also italicized within the body of the text.

OUTLINE FOR TEACHING

1. BEGIN WITH PRAYER. Learning to be a follower when you are training

to be a leader during the college years will not be easy. Only as you call upon the power of prayer as you participate in or lead each session will you be able to grasp the full meaning of each session. Pray:

for yourself

for participants

for the leader, if in a group study

for clarity of mind and spirit

for discovering your own method of following and how this book can help you to to become a followologist for others who are following you as you develop your spiritual walk

for those who will encounter you and ask for directions on how to follow

2. INTRODUCE THE CHAPTER TITLE AND TOPIC.

3. PRESENT THE CASE STUDY. This might be done by a student reading the study or giving their version of what the case study was about (enlist these people at least one week ahead).

4. ASK FOR COMMENTS OR QUESTIONS RELATED TO THE PERSONAL STUDY. If students have no comments or questions, be prepared to go to the Chat Room section for direction to stimulate discussion. Remember, in a small group setting, discussion is the desired form of communication.

5. IDENTIFY THE "FOLLOWOLOGY PRINCIPLE" AND THE "FOLLOWOLOGY BARRIER" beginning with chapter two and those in the remaining chapters. Ask how these apply to the lives of those within the group.

6. CONCLUDE WITH A REVIEW OF THE PRINCIPLE AND BARRIER and ask students to be conscious throughout the coming week of how these two elements of followology impact their lives.

7. CONCLUDE THE SESSION WITH PRAYER for openness, awareness, and development of relationships with those you are following and those who are following you.

Chapter 1
(Following a Leader You Cannot See)

INDIVIDUAL STUDY

1. Look in the Introduction and find the twenty-four followisms. At this point, which one intrigues you the most? Be ready to share your answer.

2. Read the case study in Chapter 1 and enter the Chat Room. Do you feel like Jaime? Why? Why not?

3. In the section "Following A Person" there is a text box. Have you ever felt like the disciples?

4. Give a one-sentence description of what each section addresses in our spiritual journey:

See the Leader? I Can't Even Get Online

The Decision Is to Decide

Different Types of Following

Following for Good

God's Onscreen Help

Calling Technical Support

I Want a Real Person Who Has Patience with Me

I Want to Listen to a Real Person

What Would Jesus Do?

What elements do each have in common with the others? Why? List two or three.

5. Examine the last Chat Room. It deals with a law of followology. Do you agree with the followism?
❏ Yes ❏ No ❏ Maybe
❏ Does it describe your relationship with Jesus Christ?

GROUP STUDY

1. Pick one or more Chat Room sections and spend time allowing students to share their answers and thoughts.

2. In the section dealing with "Calling Technical Support" there is a

humorous dialog presented. Ask your students to examine the dialog. Ask: How does this reflect our spiritual lives?

3. Ask students to turn to the section "I Want to Listen to a Real Person" and discuss the ways God speaks to ordinary people. Ask if they have others they want to suggest. Write these down on a large tear sheet or chalkboard for all to see.
4. Discuss followism #21: The better you know the leader, the easier it is to trust the leader." Ask your group why this would be true.
5. If you have time, ask several students to give their one-line descriptions for each of the sections in Chapter 1. Discuss why these sections are important for each person.

Chapter 2
(Following the One Who Knows the Way)

INDIVIDUAL STUDY

1. Read the case study about Alexandra. Have you ever been in a similar situation? How did that make you feel? Check out the Chat Room and answer the questions.
2. In this chapter, we begin with the **"Followology Principle"** and the **"Followology Barrier."** Memorize both of these. Remember, you can find them on the beginning page of the chapter.
3. You will find in this chapter a story concerning driver's education. Would you say you have greater respect for an "expert in his or her field" or less respect? Why?
4. Check the CrossSeekers icon in the "review" section on p. 36. Think about why that icon is located at this paragraph.

GROUP STUDY

1. Make a poster or some type of visual with the **Followology Principle** and **Followology Barrier** and place them where students can see them easily.
2. Ask students: What was your initial

response to following the one who knows the way? Ask if they feel Alexandra was better off doing her own thing. Why? Why Not?

3. Locate the two CrossSeekers icons in this chapter. They are strategically located. Ask the students to discuss why they are located where they are. How does the text reflect one seeking after the cross?
4. Ask students to examine Jeremiah 29:13 and discuss it before you leave.
5. Close in prayer.

Chapter 3
(Following by Choice with Pride Aside)

INDIVIDUAL STUDY

1. Memorize the **Followology Principle** and the **Followology Barrier** at the beginning of your study of this chapter.
2. Examine the case study carefully. Do you feel Tim made the "right" decision?
   ❏ Yes ❏ No ❏ Maybe
   Why? Why Not?
3. Look at the quote, "A defining moment occurs. Before the choice, you are not following. After the choice, you are following." Is this a significant statement for you? Think about it.
4. In the section dealing with spiritual pride, what do you think of the captain of the ship? What do you think of the one who was talking to the captain?
5. Which would you rather be in life, like the captain, or the person talking to the captain? Think about your response!

GROUP STUDY

1. Make a poster or some type of visual with the **Followology Principle** and **Followology Barrier** and place them where students can see them easily. Ask students to share their impressions of the meaning of: The Choice Principle describes our responsibility to follow. Ask them to

discuss the barrier issue of: Spiritual Pride (Followers acknowledge that they need their leaders).

2. Look at each of the Chat Room boxes and pick one or two for the students to discuss.
3. Have the students locate and discuss the CrossSeekers icons and text boxes within this chapter.
4. On a chalkboard or tear sheet, have students list some areas of spiritual pride they need to deal with in their own lives. Have a student read Jeremiah 29:13. Discuss with the students how this verse applies to the issue of spiritual pride.

Chapter 4
(Following as Learner among Learners)

INDIVIDUAL STUDY

1. Memorize the **Followology Principle** and the **Followology Barrier** at the beginning of your study of this chapter.
2. Examine the case study carefully. Which person would you be more like in a crisis—Dana or Steven? Which one is following as a learner among learners? Why?
3. The example of the Honda car points out that we must stay focused. Think of two examples during school when you have been rewarded because you remained focused.
4. When you read the quote, "Now we look at a subtle but dangerous barrier to following Jesus—comparing ourselves to other followers," have you found yourself doing this? Read on in the barrier section to discover what you can do about it.
5. The CrossSeekers icon is located next to an exercise to emphasize how close you are to following other people rather than Jesus. Make sure to check it out.

GROUP STUDY

1. Make posters or some type of visual with the **Followology Principle** and **Followology Barrier** for this week

and place them where they can be seen easily. Ask the students to share their impressions of the principles for this week.

2. Break into small groups of 4-5 and ask students to examine the case study and the Chat Box following the case study. In their small groups, have them come up with which one was a learner among learners and four reasons why. When all groups have completed the assignment, have them share with the large group.
3. Notice the various CrossSeekers icons, text boxes, and Chat Room information in this chapter. Assign various ones to small groups to study. Then have each group share their icon, text box, etc. and what they discovered, but do it through verbal means.
4. Ask the students to share the followology principle and then lead a discussion of what it means to stay focused. Ask them to discuss why this would be considered a basic discipline of following.
5. Have one or more students prepared to discuss some implications of why it is dangerous for our spiritual growth to compare ourselves to other followers. Ask them to share some examples from their lives to stimulate discussion among the larger group.
6. Close in prayer.

Chapter 5
(Following with Adjusting Expectations)

INDIVIDUAL STUDY

1. Memorize the **Followology Principle** and the **Followology Barrier** at the beginning of your study of this chapter.
2. Examine the case study carefully. In what ways are you like Kim? In what ways are you different? Where do you think God fit into Kim's actions?
3. Make sure you complete each Chat Room exercise for both the principle and the barrier. Have you tried to go

onto the web and make contact with other students? Check it out at www.crossseekers.org. It may help as you make adjustments in your following.

4. In the section dealing with Unrealistic Expectations, you find the CrossSeekers icon for "Integrity." Why do you suppose this icon is at this location?

5. Make sure you complete the last Chat Box in this chapter. What adjustments are you making to follow Jesus?

GROUP STUDY

1. Make a poster or some type of visual with the **Followology Principle and Followology Barrier** for this week. Display it where it can be seen. If you have done this for the previous weeks, put them all on a bulletin board where they can be seen week after week.

2. Have the students look at the case study. (This can be photocopied with permission, if a visitor does not have a book.) In small groups of 4-5 students, ask them to identify some major issues taking place in Kim's experience. Ask them to jot the issues down on tear sheets or with paper and pencil. When they have finished, ask each small group to share with the large group what they felt were major issues.

3. The statement is made, "In a way, the Adjustment Principle is about imitation." Ask the students to define "imitation." What are some reasons they would want to imitate Jesus?

4. Lead students to identify some "strings" they attach in order to follow Jesus.

5. Ask the students to examine the last paragraph in the chapter and the contents of the Chat Room. Ask them to share what adjustments they are willing to make based on their answers in the Chat Room.

6. Close in prayer.

Chapter 6
(Following Comes Naturally)

INDIVIDUAL STUDY

1. Memorize the **Followology Principle** and the **Followology Barrier** at the beginning of your study of this chapter.

2. Read carefully the case study. Ask yourself these questions after reading it:

> Did Chuck do the right thing in giving the interns more responsibility?
> How do you think the interns did with their task? What would you have done differently?

3. Think about the followism, "Following builds relationships." Have you discovered this with your experience? Whom do you have the best relationship with? Do you find yourself following that person's lead many times?

4. Look at the various text boxes and CrossSeekers icons within the chapter. At each one, try to understand why they are located where they are. Think about how they impact your journey of faith and your desire to be a followologist.

5. Read the section dealing with "Jesus' Discipleship Exam." After looking at the various tests, go to the Chat Room and complete what is asked in this section.

GROUP STUDY

1. Make a poster or some type of visual with the **Followology Principle** and **Followology Barrier** for this week. Display it where it can be seen. Have you put each of the principles and barriers up for students to see them week after week in your study room? If you have, call attention to each one to reinforce them for students to memorize.

2. If you have been stressing memorization, ask one or more of the students to share with the large group what they have memorized.

3. Check the Chat Boxes, the CrossSeekers icons, and the text

boxes as points of discussion.

4. Under the section dealing with the barrier, "The Barrier of Misunderstanding the Purpose of Testing," note the various types of testing offered the disciples. Have the students divide into small groups. Assign each group a different type of test and ask them to examine the scripture associated with that test. Give them time to share among themselves. Ask for a report from each group dealing with the type test they had. Ask them to think of how that type test is given to Christians today.

5. Go back to the case study. Ask the students to share how the relationship principle is a key to being a followologist.

6. Close with prayer.

Chapter 7
(Following on Purpose)

INDIVIDUAL STUDY

1. Memorize the **Followology Principle** and the **Followology Barrier** at the beginning of your study of this chapter.

2. Read the case study carefully. Is Brandon's situation all that big a deal? How did you relate to what his professor, Dr. Anderson, told him at the end of the case study?

3. This chapter deals first with "change." In what ways do you think your life is changed because you have decided to be a followologist?

4. The chapter also deals with the element of "failure." We all have failed. Look at the section dealing with Michael Jordan. Can you believe it?

5. Simon Peter is often admired because we know where he has been and we have seen what God did with his failure. Look at the things Peter did. Which one would describe where you are spiritually as you follow Jesus?

GROUP STUDY

1. Make a poster or some type of visu-

al with the **Followology Principle** and **Followology Barrier** for this week. This session deals with change and failure.

2. Ask someone in advance to be prepared to share the gist of the case study. Ask the group to share their reaction to what has happened in Brandon's life. You may even want to break them into small groups of 4-5 to share reactions. If so, have a large-group share time where each group can share different reactions.

3. In the section titled, 'The "After" Part of "Before and After,"' find the text box quote. From Allen's paraphrase, how would you interpret for your group what it means to: "Give it your best shot, guys. We really don't have a choice in the matter"? Ask the group: What do you think he means by that quote? How does it impact who we are and what we do?

4. It's important to discuss the issue of failure. Have the group examine the elements of what happened to Simon Peter. Ask: Could this happen to you as an individual? Could it happen to us as a group? Spend some time discussing these questions.

5. Close in prayer.

Chapter 8
(Following All the Way Home)

INDIVIDUAL STUDY

1. Memorize the **Followology Principle** and the **Followology Barrier** at the beginning of your study of this chapter.

2. Read the case study carefully. Ask yourself the question, "Who is following me?" Were you surprised at Mitch's reaction? Why? Why not?

3. What is the final barrier principle? Why is it so important? How big a part does it play in your life?

4. Examine the case study of Jon. Which person would you identify with spiritually in the study?

5. What are the three things you want others who follow you to learn about Jesus?

GROUP STUDY

1. Make a poster or some type of visual with the **Followology Principle** and **Followology Barrier** for this week. The session this week deals with the destination principle, which emphasizes the reward of following and reluctant leadership. You might post this somewhere so students know what the study will be about this week.

2. Have someone prepared to read or tell the story of Jon. Divide the students into small groups. Ask each group to discuss what they consider to be the impact the seniors left on Jon. Ask them to answer the question, "What impact do we want to make on our campus for Christ?"

4. Examine the challenge and give it to the students. Ask if they are willing to form another followology group next semester. It only takes one. How would this impact the campus?

CONCLUSION

You have completed the course requirements for Followology 101-102. Congratulations! The conclusion is a wrap-up and review. Take time either individually or in a large group setting to examine once again the

Followology Principles
and
Followology Barriers.

Pray that God will provide opportunities to follow Him over the barriers which will confront you on your journey. *Keep following!*

The CrossSeekers™ Covenant

You will seek me and find me when you seek me with all your heart.
Jeremiah 29:13

As a seeker of the cross of Christ, I am called to break away from trite, nonchalant, laissez faire Christian living. I accept the challenge to divine daring, to consecrated recklessness for Christ, to devout adventure in the face of ridiculing contemporaries. Created in the image of God and committed to excellence as a disciple of Jesus Christ,

I will be a person of integrity
Do your best to present yourself to God as one approved, a workman who does not need to be ashamed and who correctly handles the word of truth. 2 Timothy 2:15

My attitudes and actions reveal my commitment to live the kind of life Christ modeled for me to speak the truth in love, to stand firm in my convictions, to be honest and trustworthy.

I will pursue consistent spiritual growth
So then, just as you received Christ Jesus as Lord, continue to live in Him, rooted and built up in Him, strengthened in the faith as you were taught, and overflowing with thankfulness. Colossians 2:6-7

The Christian life is a continuing journey, and I am committed to a consistent, personal relationship with Jesus Christ, to faithful study of His word, and to regular corporate spiritual growth through the ministry of the New Testament church.

I will speak and live a relevant, authentic, and consistent witness
Always be prepared to give an answer to everyone who asks you to give the reason for the hope that you have. 1 Peter 3:15

I will tell others the story of how Jesus changed my life, and I will seek to live a radically changed life each day. I will share the good news of Jesus Christ with courage and boldness.

I will seek opportunities to serve in Christ s name
The Spirit of the Lord is on me, because He has anointed me to preach good news to the poor. He has sent me to proclaim freedom for the prisoners and recovery of sight for the blind, to release the oppressed, to proclaim the year of the Lord s favor. Luke 4:18-19

I believe that God desires to draw all people into a loving, redeeming relationship with Him. As His disciple, I will give myself to be His hands to reach others in ministry and missions.

I will honor my body as the temple of God, dedicated to a lifestyle of purity
Do you not know that your body is a temple of the Holy Spirit, who is in you, whom you have received from God? You are not your own; you were bought at a price. Therefore honor God with your body. 1 Corinthians 6:19-20

Following the example of Christ, I will keep my body healthy and strong, avoiding temptations and destructive personal vices. I will honor the gift of life by keeping myself sexually pure and free from addictive drugs.

I will be godly in all things, Christlike in all relationships
Therefore, as God s chosen people, holy and dearly loved, clothe yourselves with compassion, kindness, humility, gentleness, and patience. Bear with each other and forgive what grievances you may have against one another. Forgive as the Lord forgave you. And over all these virtues put on love, which binds them all together in perfect unity. Colossians 3:12-14

In every relationship and in every situation, I will seek to live as Christ would. I will work to heal brokenness, to value each person as a child of God, to avoid petty quarrels and harsh words, to let go of bitterness and resentment that hinder genuine Christian love.

Covenant Resources
To order any of these resources, call toll free 1-800-458-2772.

CROSS
SEEKERS

• Discipleship Covenant for a New Generation
by Richard Blackaby and Henry Blackaby
How do the principles of the Covenant guide us to live committed to following Jesus? This interactive study provides biblical information needed to be a CrossSeeker. ISBN 07673.90849 • $8.95

I will pursue consistent spiritual growth.
• God's Invitation: A Challenge
  to College Students
by Henry Blackaby & Richard Blackaby
Through an interactive study focusing on application of the principles found in *Experiencing God*, students learn how these principles radically impact the daily issues of collegiate life. Seven sessions, 35 individual Bible studies. ISBN 08054 9679 3 • $9.95

I will speak and live a relevant, authentic, and consistent witness.
• Into Their Shoes: Helping the Lost
  Find Christ
by John Kramp & Allen Jackson
By seeing life as non-believers do, collegians are challenged to move from confrontational gospel showdowns to relational in-their-shoes empathy. Each session includes interactive Bible study and group exercises. Helpful teaching suggestions are included for leaders. ISBN 08054 9769 2 • $9.95

I will be godly in all things, Christlike in all relationships.
• Discover the Winning Edge
by William Mitchell & Jerry Pounds
Through interactive study of six proven principles for developing godly self-esteem, students are challenged to develop positive hablts, overcome fears, set goals, and rely on the strength Christ provides to discover the winning edge in life. ISBN 07673 3178 8 • $9.95
I will be a person of integrity.

• Out of the Moral Maze: Setting You Free to
  Make Right Choices
by Josh McDowell
Through group sessions and individual activities, students learn truth to apply to every moral dilemma of life. Workbook includes all teaching materials. ISBN 08054 9832 X • $11.95

I will honor my body as the temple of God, dedicated to a lifestyle of purity.
• Faithful and True: Sexual Integrity in
  a Fallen World
by Mark R. Laaser
Where in our culture does a person go to develop a healthy and Christ-honoring attitude and lifestyle concerning sexuality? How can Christians and the church respond to a world gone sexually mad? This book seeks to answer these questions. ISBN 08054 9819 2 • $12.95

I will seek opportunities to serve in Christ's name.
• Meeting Needs, Sharing Christ: Ministry
  Evangelism in Today's New Testament Church
by Don Atkinson and Charles Roesel
Leads individuals and churches to understand the concept and capture the vision for ministry evangelism, identify needs, and minister to broken lives in the community. Six-week small-group study. ISBN 08054 9840 0 • $6.95   ISBN 08054 9841 9

• Transitions: Preparing for College
compiled by Art Herron
Designed for the high school junior/senior preparing for college. Written to answer many questions you may have about college...and how to begin the process of becoming a CrossSeeker in your junior/senior years. Practical helps such as the "time line" keep you on track.
ISBN 07673 9082 2 • $7.95 (Student Version)

To order any of these resources, call toll free 1-800-458-2772.